# THE PEDAGOGY AND PRACTICE OF WESTERN-TRAINED CHINESE ENGLISH LANGUAGE TEACHERS

Providing an East-West flow of language teaching knowledge and know-how to balance prevailing Western-centric perspectives, this book is an in-depth investigation of the impact of Western-based language teacher education on the pedagogy and practice of Chinese English language teachers who received their training in Western institutions  or those that emphasize Western-based teaching approaches. A significant and growing number of these teachers will influence millions of language learners on China's mainland over the next decades.

*The Pedagogy and Practice of Western-Trained Chinese English Language Teachers*
- Forefronts Chinese teachers' voices and experiences in the context of their workplaces and classrooms
- Provides accounts from teachers who are able to describe,  to critique, and to navigate the two sides of their experiences as Chinese professionals trained abroad
- Connects and balances theory and practice—explains the sociocultural lens used to view the teachers' experiences and shows classroom-based events and teaching activities in socioculturally situated and localized contexts
- Discusses the Chinese government's policies on the training of teachers and analyzes them in terms of their impact on both American and Chinese higher education institutions

An important resource for language educators interested in examining the impact of teacher training on Chinese teachers of English who have studied abroad, this book  is a "must read" for anyone interested in teaching theories and practices adopted from the West and applied within an Asian setting.

**Pu Hong** is Associate Professor of Linguistics and Language Education and Vice President, Qujing Normal University, China.

**Faridah Pawan** is Associate Professor in the Department of Literacy, Culture and Language Education, School of Education, Indiana University, USA.

## ESL & Applied Linguistics Professional Series
### Eli Hinkel, Series Editor

| Hinkel | *Teaching Academic ESL Writing: Practical Techniques in Vocabulary and Grammar* |
| Hinkel/Fotos, Eds. | *New Perspectives on Grammar Teaching in Second Language Classrooms* |
| Hinkel | *Second Language Writers' Text: Linguistic and Rhetorical Features* |

Visit **www.routledge.com/education**
for additional information on titles
in the ESL & Applied Linguistics Professional Series

# THE PEDAGOGY AND PRACTICE OF WESTERN-TRAINED CHINESE ENGLISH LANGUAGE TEACHERS

## Foreign Education, Chinese Meanings

*Pu Hong and Faridah Pawan*

Routledge
Taylor & Francis Group

NEW YORK AND LONDON

First published 2014
by Routledge
711 Third Avenue, New York, NY 10017

and in the UK
by Routledge
2 Park Square, Milton Park, Abingdon, Oxon OX14 4RN

*Routledge is an imprint of the Taylor & Francis Group, an informa business*

*Library of Congress Cataloging in Publication Data*
Pu, Hong, 1972–
    The pedagogy and practice of Western-trained Chinese English language teachers :
    foreign education, Chinese meanings / Hong Pu, Faridah Pawan.
    pages cm. — (ESL & Applied Linguistics Professional series)
    1. English language—Study and teaching—Chinese speakers. 2. English
    teachers—In-service training—China. 3. English teachers, Training of—China.
    4. Education—United States. I. Pawan, Faridah. II. Title.
    PE1068.C5P8 2013
    428.0071'051—dc23
    2013017103

ISBN: 978-0-415-62935-5 (hbk)
ISBN: 978-0-415-62936-2 (pbk)
ISBN: 978-0-203-09518-8 (ebk)

Typeset in Bembo and Stone Sans
by EvS Communication Networx, Inc.

Printed and bound in the United States of America by Publishers Graphics,
LLC on sustainably sourced paper.

We dedicate this book to all our students who teach
and inspire us every day.

# CONTENTS

# PREFACE

The demand for English language teaching worldwide has grown by 300% in the past five years. There is a large investment on the part of many governments to internationalize their educational systems by introducing English into their schools. This is particularly the case in East Asia, including China, the homeland of the English teachers described in this book. For example, in Korea and Japan, there are now national mandates for teachers to teach their subject areas in English beginning at the elementary level. Consequently, there is a rush to get teachers from these areas trained and qualified by sending them abroad, particularly to Western countries. Thus, this book specifically looks at the impact of this decision and consequently will be of interest to the individuals and institutions involved.

We also had the English-as-a-second language/foreign language (ESL/EFL) teaching community in mind when we wrote this book, including graduates and undergraduates planning to become language teachers, language teachers already on the job, language teacher educators, language planning and policy makers, and language education publishers. Along with the focus on teachers' voices and insider perspectives on the impact of Western education on Chinese English language teachers, these readers will also find emerging and hot button topics in the field such as the relevancy of Western language teacher education; the greater number of nonnative English language teachers in comparison to native speakers; the role of language teachers and teaching in the postmethod era; and governmental policies that support and obstruct progress in language teaching and learning.

Finally, we also focus on theoretical and experientially based perspectives. For those interested in bridging pedagogical theory and teaching practice, we demonstrate how the sociocultural lens allows for a narrowing of the gap between the two. We also share our perspectives based on the backgrounds we have in common with the teachers discussed in the book, namely, as individuals from the East who were educated in the West and who returned home as professionals to institutions in our respective countries (Faridah Pawan, however, accepted a U.S. faculty position seven years after returning home to Malaysia). Thus, along with the teachers, we are able to provide empathetic and informed perspectives on the "dual vision" that results from such experiences. In doing so, we hope to contribute to an East–West flow of language teaching knowledge and know-how to balance prevailing Western-centric perspectives on second and foreign language teaching.

# ACKNOWLEDGMENTS

We first thank all the teachers we have worked alongside. We are indebted to them for their generosity in sharing their thoughts, ideas, views, opinions, and materials with us. Most of all, we are grateful to them for allowing us to be a part of their classrooms so that we could observe and learn from their instructional expertise. Xiè xiè nǐ.

We also thank Naomi Silverman, Editor/Publisher and Eli Hinkel, Applied Linguistics Series Editor, at Routledge/Taylor & Francis for their gentle support and guidance, which provided us with room to explore and reach deeper into our ideas.

Thank you to the group of energetic people in our respective departments who were willing to lend a hand whenever we needed them as they followed our writing progress. We especially thank Zhong Wei (Vina) for the insights and advice she shared with us. Thank you as well to Li Yan and Kou Ying from Yunnan Province, and IU's graduate students G. Yeon Park, Mateus Yumarnamto, and Ai Chu Ding for chasing after runaway references.

We extend also our gratitude to our colleague, Sharon Pugh, whom we suspect was a feline in a previous life, whose sharp eyes and editorial "claws" put the fear of long-windedness into our hearts and minds.

Finally, we are grateful to Gou Yongming, Gou Yiran, Gou Yiyi, Charles, Joshua, and Samuel for their unwavering faith in all that we do. Thank you for being forever willing to go on "wild rides" with us, over and over again!

**Pu Hong and Faridah Pawan**

# 1

# INTRODUCTION

*Experiences and learning are treasures we carry with us everywhere.*

The main purpose of this book is to allow teachers' own voices to provide insights into the professional lives of Chinese English language teachers who received their training in the West or at other overseas institutions that emphasize Western-based teaching approaches. More specifically, the book reports an in-depth investigation of (a) the impact of Western-based language teacher education on Chinese English language teachers; (b) the agency and efforts the teachers undertook to take ownership of their Western education in their pedagogies and practices at home; (c) the nature of English-language policy and instruction in China; and (d) the relevance of the lessons learned from this investigation for language teacher education programs that prepare students for university assignments abroad.

In China today, there are approximately 440 to 650 million users and learners of English (He & Zhang, 2010), outnumbering the entire U.S. population and reflecting the status of English as a world language. Not surprisingly, therefore, English language teaching has become a key strategy for China to achieve modernization and global economic success. As a result, a growing number of Chinese students who go abroad to study are English language teachers pursuing graduate degrees, many of whom return to become language education leaders at their home institutions and join a broad, concerted effort to elevate the quality of instruction in Chinese universities.

These Chinese teachers of English as a second/foreign language are part of a worldwide phenomenon that has emerged in the profession. Teachers who are nonnative speakers of English (NNESTs) now comprise the majority of the workforce (80%) in English-language classrooms across the globe (Braine,

2010). This predominance is dramatically illustrated by comparing the number of Chinese English language teachers (2 million; Braine, 2010) to the number of certified U.S. teachers of English (150,000; Quality Counts, 2009), a quarter of whom are themselves nonnative speakers of English. This phenomenon can be explained in part by the inexorable spread of English as a global language and falling birth rates in English-speaking countries (Lagabaster & Sierra, 2004). According to Graddol (2001), 9% of the world's population grew up speaking English as a mother tongue in the mid-20th century, while only 5% will do so in the mid-21st century.

The enrollment trends of many graduate language teacher education programs in the United States and other English-speaking countries provide additional evidence. For example, Brady and Gulikers (2004) report that as many as 80 to 90% of the students enrolled in master's level Teachers of English to Speakers of Other Languages (TESOL) programs in American universities from 1998 to 2001 were nonnative speakers of English, most of whom were from non-Western countries. When such students return home, they become pioneers at their universities, seeking ways to negotiate the cross-cultural transfer of their Western-based teacher training into local English-language education programs. Understanding the outcomes of their Western language teacher education programs is essential not only for the improvement of these international students' preparation in the West, but also for the development of the institutions that send them.

This book is thus important for two reasons. First, by employing a sociocultural approach, it provides an in-depth look into the empowering but also challenging impact of Western education on Chinese English language teaching professionals who return home. There is little research in the literature that addresses the relevant issues, particularly how Western-trained international language teachers resituate themselves as professionals in their home environments after years away. One result of this research gap is that scant attention has been paid to designing Western-based teacher education programs that serve the needs of international students preparing to teach in and manage programs in non-Western settings in which the cultural background and pedagogical expectations of students, educators, and government officials may be quite different. This book addresses this deficit by providing a direct view into the experiences of Chinese teachers through their own reflections on their experiences as learners in the West, their knowledge of the social contexts of their workplaces, and the teaching and learning processes in their own Chinese classrooms. By taking this close-up perspective, the book provides a microcosmic study of the sociocultural processes of institutional change and development undertaken to transform the landscape of Chinese higher education and make it more competitive with universities in the West. In this way, the book can also serve as a resource for the design and implementation of language education graduate programs in the United States and other English-speaking countries that prepare teachers for overseas university assignments.

The second purpose of this book is to provide a case study of Chinese teachers' efforts to localize their Western education for use in Chinese classrooms. To this end, the authors directly address the disjuncture between teacher professional development programs and teaching practices that is of major concern in the field. Even when the focus is on Western institutions, there are substantial gaps between theory and practice, goals and outcomes, and the ideal and the real (e.g., Korthagen, 2001; Stigmar, 2010). When Western-based teaching frameworks are introduced to classrooms abroad, the "translation" of concepts and pedagogies into non-Western practices can be presumed to be even more complex and challenging. The book thus demonstrates "pathways of practice" (Pawan & Groff Thomalla, 2005) for localizing Western pedagogy in Chinese classrooms and serves as a guide for future studies on the localization of teaching in diverse settings.

## Unique Features

To meet these goals, the book provides the following unique features:

- *Teacher "insider" perspectives on the impact of language teacher training in a country currently of high international interest*: As mentioned above, Chinese educators' voices and experiences in the contexts of their workplaces are brought to the forefront and thus provide an insider perspective.
- *East meets West teacher perspectives*: The book is also unique in that it includes perspectives of teachers who are able to describe, critique, and navigate the two sides of their experiences as Chinese professionals trained abroad. Understanding the relevance of Chinese culture in language teacher training and how its realities shape the professional development of overseas-trained Chinese teachers will enlighten educators dealing with similar complexities in other settings.
- *Connection and balance between theory and practice*: The authors will take readers through the interpretive and reflective aspects of the sociocultural view they used to focus on the teachers' experiences. The book will also provide classroom-based events and teaching activities that emerge when instruction is socioculturally situated and localized in ways that are meaningful to Chinese teachers and students alike.
- *Updates on Chinese teachers' professional development rules and regulations in China*: The Chinese government's policies on the training of teachers abroad will be analyzed in terms of their impact on both American and Chinese tertiary institutions, thus shedding light on ways to analyze political as well as cultural influences that impact higher education.

## Overview

In chapter 2 ("Situated and 'Glocalized' Understanding"), we begin by discussing our sociocultural theoretical perspective and stance. We explain how the "sociocultural turn" (Johnson, 2006) that the language teacher education field has taken is timely and defines current interest in the field. In particular, this chapter makes clear how we use Freeman and Johnson's (1998) sociocultural framework for understanding the teacher knowledge base as well as activity theory as analytical lenses to describe and explain the resources that Chinese English language teachers draw upon to project and sustain their professional expertise.

In chapter 3 ("Hits and Misses"), we take a critical perspective on the experiences of international students who study abroad to become language teachers or teacher educators. This perspective provides a rationale for the importance of the information and insights we provide. In particular we focus on the discrepancies between their training and the realities they face when they return home. This chapter also identifies current thinking and emerging reforms that have the potential to improve the situation, including the importance of teachers' sense of teaching plausibility (Prabhu, 1990), advocacy for a "post-method era" (Kumaradivelu, 2006a), and the recognition that effective teaching is defined by its contextual responsiveness.

We provide an overview of the larger context of English language teaching in China in chapter 4 ("Evolving Landscapes"). In this chapter, we undertake an overview of Chinese English-language educators' and policy makers' positions on communicative language teaching (CLT) since 1984. They include acceptance of CLT as an indicator of progress that could overcome English language teaching that results in students being educated in grammar and vocabulary, but not being able to make themselves understood in English or being able to understand spoken English; resistance to CLT as a foreign imposition on Chinese culture and epistemic traditions; and the adaptation and inclusion of CLT as part of the eclectic strategy to reform education. We also describe Western-trained Chinese teachers' efforts to localize CLT, an emerging trend that prioritizes place-based teaching knowledge and practice that is context- and community-specific.

In chapter 5, "The Middle Kingdom and Beyond," we describe Chinese teachers' pathways to professional development overseas. In this chapter, we provide a closer look at Chinese teachers who have gone abroad and why they chose or were chosen to do so. In doing so, we describe the various opportunities and pathways available to Chinese English language teachers to pursue education outside China. We also include information from interviews with Chinese teachers as to their views on overseas education and its relevance to the current Chinese educational climate.

In chapter 6 ("Light and Heat"), we focus on the multifaceted ways in which Chinese teachers have been impacted by their overseas training. In particular, we describe how the teachers felt empowered and strengthened by their acquisition of knowledge that had been foreign to them. Also, our description includes how the teachers' overseas training enabled them to see the strengths of their Chinese knowledge and training, thereby validating their preexisting expertise. Finally, we describe personal and professional challenges the teachers faced as a consequence of what was perceived to be their privileged but foreign training.

In chapter 7 ("Taking Ownership"), we use activity theory to trace how the Western-based communicative language teaching (CLT) approach was being localized by these Chinese teachers. Specifically, we identify four phases of localization: namely, the teachers' appropriation or ownership of specific concepts of CLT; the materials (conceptual and practical) that consequently mediated their instruction; the tensions and contradictions that emerged; and the resulting changes in their instruction.

In chapter 8 we analyze the Chinese government's 12th (and latest) 5-year plan for National Economic and Social Development (NESD) (2011–2015) and the Outline of the National Long-Term and Short-Term Education Reform and Development Plan (2010–2020) for educational reform (2010) and their impact on the professional development of university teachers. The title of this chapter, "Changing from Earth to Sky," indicates the major and ever-evolving changes taking place in teacher education and professional development in China as these directly impact the roles of Western-trained teachers. The national plan calls specifically for the internationalization of not only the curriculum but teachers' professional development as well. We also provide insight into the programmatic changes that are taking place in the training of teachers in a Chinese normal university (i.e., a university for training teachers rather than for research alone) in response to the plan, particularly with regard to the training of language teachers overseas. We end our discussion by reflecting on how our findings might inform teacher training programs in China and the United States. We also suggest a professional development model.

Whereas the core of the book focuses on the impact on their professional lives of the Chinese English language teachers' Western education, in chapter 9, the final chapter, we present the teachers' reflections on what this educational experience has meant to each of them in personal terms. In this sense, the Western education that the teachers received was made meaningful by the way they interpreted it in the context of their experiences not only as educators but also as individuals.

## Why We Wrote This Book

Coauthors, Pu Hong and Faridah Pawan came together to write this book as their interests in language teaching and language teacher education converged. Below, each of us describes the major experiences that shaped her perspectives in the writing of this book. We both believe that effective instruction is grounded in the sociocultural context in which the instruction takes place. We thus work to validate and bring to the surface teachers' knowledge base that has been informed and transformed by the communities and settings in which they live and work.

Pu Hong started her career as an English language teacher in Kunming, China. She then pursued graduate education in Australia and a doctorate in language education in the United States. Currently, Pu Hong is a Vice President and associate professor of linguistics at Qu Jing University in Yunnan Province. Faridah Pawan was an English language teacher in Malaysia before pursuing higher education in the US. After receiving her doctorate, she became a faculty member at Universiti Malaya in Kuala Lumpur and then returned to the US, where she is currently an associate professor of Literacy, Culture, and Language Education in the School of Education at Indiana University, Bloomington, Indiana.

### Pu Hong

As a Chinese educator who for 14 years has been intensely engaged in both English teaching and pre- and in-service English teacher training at all levels, I have always focused on one particular question: How can I really help the large population of Chinese English language teachers, even just a little? In my work, I have encountered various concerns about the effectiveness of English-teacher training programs. I have witnessed many teachers suffering in top-down English teaching reforms who have struggled to link theories to their day-to-day practices. I am also much concerned that Chinese English language teacher education programs are obsessed with methods-driven curricula and largely ignore what teachers really must consider in classroom decision making, and, as Crandall (2000) observes, what knowledge and beliefs they bring to their teaching from their own learning experiences. G. Hu (2005) has described the woeful state of preservice English teacher training programs:

> With few exceptions, pre-service teacher education programs suffer from outdated curriculums and teaching content, a narrow focus on language proficiency at the expense of educational work, a marginalization of school-based work, an inadequately defined knowledge base for teaching, and a teacher-dominated, textbook-based, transmission-oriented pedagogy that severs language proficiency work from pedagogical preparation.
> *(p. 19)*

Facing this situation, I firmly believe that the concept of "pedagogy glocalization" can empower Chinese English language teachers, including myself, by pushing us beyond methods and liberating us from the practice of "self-marginalization" (Kumaravadivelu, 2006a). This self-marginalization is largely due to "the widespread acceptance of the superiority of Western methods over local practices" (Kumaravadivelu, 2006a, p. 219). When it comes to teaching English as foreign language, many program administrators, teacher educators, and classroom teachers in China have become accustomed to surrendering to the visible and invisible power of Western-based teaching methods, textbooks, media, and even native speakers of English. I feel it is urgent and also my responsibility to help my colleagues to realize their capabilities and strengths by exploring how Chinese English language teachers make their own sense of their teaching and how they can glocalize Western-based pedagogy according to their specific contexts. The process of exploring the glocalization of Chinese English language teachers' pedagogy will itself help teachers step away from searching for the best teaching method and learn how to be sensitive to "teaching a particular group of learners pursuing a particular set of goals within a particular institutional context embedded in a particular sociocultural milieu" (Kumaravadivelu, 2001, p. 538).

### *Faridah Pawan*

My professional experiences in Malaysia and the United States define my position. For example, as English language teachers and teacher educators in Malaysia with doctorates from the West, my colleagues and I were constantly subjected to overseas evaluators who would jet in and jet out of our classrooms, assessing the effectiveness of our teaching based on the short period of time they were there and on methods and standards set elsewhere. We also experienced multiple English-language policies throughout our lives as students and educators, from English as a standalone subject (1969–1983), to English as a medium of instruction in engineering, medical, and technical areas in higher education and private institutions (1993 onwards), to English through the content of science and mathematics in public schools (2003 onwards), and finally to a reversal of policies back to English as a language to be taught only as a subject (2012 onwards). In these changing situations, teachers were caught in the middle trying to address a moving target of expectations and responsibilities. Our saving grace was to subscribe to what Prabhu calls "a sense of plausibility" (1990, p. 161), whereby our search was not for the best teaching method out there but rather for ways to teach responsively based on what we knew about our students, our setting, and ourselves. In this regard, we aimed for teaching that was "active, alive, and operational enough to create a sense of involvement in both the teacher and the student" (p. 173).

In the United States, as a faculty member, I struggle with what I see often as the "voices from the margins" (Kubota, 1998, p. 394), most acutely when working with international students who are developing their careers as educators. Their theoretical and pedagogical experiences often differ from those of their U.S. colleagues, and having their perspectives relegated to the periphery negates their credibility and ignores their responsibility as responsive and effective teachers to assume mind-sets and undertake approaches that are different from current dominant Western perspectives. Unfortunately, those who assert their own valid though alternative points of view are often silenced or harshly criticized as "traditionalists" (Kubota, 1998, p. 404).

Additionally, as a teacher educator in the United States, I am cognizant that a significant aspect of an English language teacher's job is to advocate for his or her students, most of whom are newcomers to the country. In turn, I see my role as an advocate for English language teachers, particularly in bringing about recognition for their expertise and contribution to students' learning. This role is important because these teachers in public schools are often not credited with having their own legitimate expertise but are viewed solely as providers of support for other classroom and content area teachers. The latter, moreover, are often given the credit when English-language students do well while their teachers are held responsible for failing to bridge the achievement gap when the students fail. The fact that these teachers have a grounded and specific knowledge base to move students from learning the language to using it to learn is too often lost amidst schools' scramble to demonstrate achievement in a short period of time through scores on standardized tests. Thus, drawing on my experiences in both Malaysia and the United States, I take it as my mission to bring to the fore not only the teachers' voices but also an accurate understanding of their professionalism and the circumstances under which they do their work as a means of validating their perspectives and expertise.

My connection to teachers in China has been nurtured by my collaboration with dedicated colleagues and teachers from three universities there as well as equally talented and passionate doctoral students from several Chinese provinces. My multiple trips to collaborate in research and teaching with my Chinese colleagues and students have given me an appreciation for both the opportunities and complexities in the lives of Chinese language teachers and teacher educators trained in West.

In sum, our combined professional experiences in China, the United States, and Malaysia as second language pedagogical researchers and practitioners have served to shape our perspectives. They have also stimulated the interest and provided the motivation for us to collaborate in this book.

# 2

# SITUATED AND "GLOCALIZED" UNDERSTANDING

## Using Sociocultural Perspectives as Lenses

*Crossing the river by feeling the stones.*

As coauthors, we have been influenced by the Vygotskian-inspired sociocultural perspective. In particular, we take the position that our own learning and development are informed and transformed by our experiences in the communities in which we work and live. From this position, we see teachers' knowledge as by nature place-based in that it is rooted in the context in which they teach. We also view teachers' knowledge as emerging out of socially mediated activities and in their engagement with others. Also, from our point of view, teachers' agency is critical as they are active constructors of their teaching knowledge. Finally, we subscribe to the concept of "glocalization," by which the focus is on reframing "global" teaching approaches and trends to address the exigencies of local contexts. These positions will be evident throughout this book, particularly when we delve into the lives of the Western educated Chinese English language teachers. We discuss each of the viewpoints that have informed and continue to influence us in our research and our outlook as teachers, teacher educators, and coauthors of this book.

## The Importance of Context and Social Engagement

Vygotsky (1978) argued that knowledge is context-dependent and mediated through social and cultural artifacts. Criticizing the concept of context-independent cognition, he stressed that people learn and develop their cognition and unique ways of thinking through participating in social activities and interacting in cultural contexts. This sociocultural perspective proposes that human thinking and behaviors cannot be understood by looking at the individual in isolation but rather in the contexts of politics, culture, and history. Johnson (2006) describes this epistemological shift as evolving "from behaviorist, to cognitive, to situated, social and distributed views of human cognition" (p. 236). She writes:

> The epistemological stance of the sociocultural turn defines human learning as a dynamic social activity that is situated in physical and social contexts, and distributed across persons, tools, and activities.
>
> *(p. 237)*

From this perspective, teacher learning and development is viewed as "life-long and emerging out of and through experiences in social contexts" (Johnson, 2006, p. 239).

The sociocultural perspective has validated the conception of teachers as "socioprofessionals" (Freeman, 2009, p. 15), whose learning and knowledge are embedded in their participation in social practices. As Freeman argues, disciplinary knowledge (language, applied linguistics, second language acquisition, literature and culture) accompanied by pedagogical knowledge of how to teach language falls short of developing the professional unless the two are situated within the interpersonal interactions and activities within the contexts in which the teaching takes place. In this regard Freeman has recast the scope of the professional development of second language teachers to encompass what he calls *substance, engagement,* and *outcomes* (p. 15). While the latter two terms refer to the evolution and consequences of teacher knowledge and professional development over time, "substance" alters the traditional conception of "content," which traditionally refers to the disciplinary skills and knowledge teachers should learn, by also including their participation in the activities within the intellectual, physical, and social settings in which learning and teaching take place.

The central constructs of sociocultural theory provide us with deeper insights into the juxtaposition of content, process, and sociocultural participation in teachers' development of their knowledge base. Johnson and Golombek (2003) argue that sociocultural theory is a useful framework to explain teacher learning in terms of three key components: (a) internalization and transformation; (b) the zone of proximal development (ZPD); and (c) mediational means. First, in terms of internalization and transformation, sociocultural theory focuses on how an individual moves back and forth between external and internal activities. In this process, internal and external regulations transform and are understood in terms of each other. Johnson and Golombek (2003) state, "Internalization involves a process in which a person's activity is initially mediated by other people or cultural artifacts but later comes to be controlled by the person as he or she appropriates resources to regulate his or her own activities" (p. 731). This social mediation occurs in what Vygotsky defined as the zone of proximal development (ZPD), which suggests that people can advance through collaboration with other more capable individuals with the help of cultural resources. Within the ZPD, mediational means include three levels: object-regulation (e.g., lesson plan), other-regulation (e.g., talking with other teachers), and self-regulation (e.g., keeping personal teaching diaries). This mediation allows teachers to experience a transformative and dialogic process in which they can progress by seeking help from outside resources and people, making adjustments in both their cognition and actions, and gaining new understandings of their work.

Mediational tools that teachers use to guide these processes of internalization and transformation comprise conceptual tools and practical tools (Grossman, Smagorinsky, & Valencia, 1999). Conceptual tools include both "broadly applicable theories" and "theoretical principles and concepts" (p. 14) that teachers use to guide their classroom practices. Practical tools are classroom practices, strategies, and resources which have more "local and immediate utility" (p. 14). Some examples of practical tools are unit plans, journal writing, and textbooks. It is therefore by studying how teachers use these tools of mediation to adjust their activities that we are able to trace teacher learning and development from the perspective of sociocultural theory, as explained by Johnson and Golombek (2003):

> It [sociocultural theory] enables teacher educators to see how various tools work to create a mediational space in which teachers can externalize their current understandings and then reconceptualize and recontextualize their understandings and develop new ways of engaging in the activities associated with teaching.
>
> *(p. 735)*

Human agency is inherent in the premise that teacher knowledge and learning are context-bound and embedded in their social practices, in particular the acknowledgment that teachers are key players in their own learning and construction of knowledge.

## The Importance of Human Agency

Ahearn (2001) provisionally refers to agency as the "socioculturally mediated capacity to act" (p. 112), capturing a person's capability, as an individual or group member, to initiate and take responsibility for an action while emphasizing how agency "mediates and is mediated by the sociocultural context" (van Lier, 2008, p. 172).

From a sociocultural perspective, agency is not only about performance but also about interpretations and significance of actions guided by personal experiences and histories. This viewpoint asserts that "learners actively engage in constructing the terms and conditions of their own learning" (Lantolf & Thorne, 2006, p. 239), which is made meaningful by their past and present circumstances. Individuals also engage in their own learning because it meets their desires, intentions, and needs, a direct link to personal motivation (Lantolf & Pavlenko, 2001). In that regard, agency is not simply a matter of social enculturation, appropriation, or accommodation of resources to existing circumstances. Who and what teachers are and how they learn are a part of their knowledge of teaching and mediate how they perceive it and its effectiveness. Teachers use their backgrounds and past experiences as a means to make sense of new information, to evaluate the worthiness of their actions, and to strategize their instruction.

Nevertheless, from the sociocultural perspective, agency is not seen as a "property" of the individual. It is a capacity for action that develops by means of relationships that are constantly being reconstructed and renegotiated "around the individual and with the society at large" (Lantolf & Pavlenko, 2001, p. 148). Taken in this light, agency cannot be equated with an individual's ultimate control in initiating action. Agency, as Lantolf and Thorne (2006) point out, is subject to contextual "constraints and affordances that make certain actions probable, others possible, and yet others impossible" (Lantolf & Thorne, 2006, p. 238).

For the authors of this book, the sociocultural perspective on agency is critical for several reasons. It supports the argument that teachers are actively involved in their own learning and acquisition of expertise. In the sociocultural framework, agency counters the view of teachers as "empty vessels waiting to be filled with theoretical and pedagogical skills" (Freeman & Johnson, 1998, p. 401); rather it acknowledges how their prior experiences in different contexts and beliefs inform their teaching theories and practices. That is, teachers are not viewed as passive knowledge consumers to be assessed by how well they implement new theories, methods, or materials furnished to them; rather the notion of agency highlights how teachers "reconstruct themselves as legitimate knowledge producers" (Shin, 2006, p.162) and as generators and theorizers of teaching knowledge in their own right (Cochran-Smith & Lytle, 1999; Johnson, 2009).

## The Lenses We Used

The sociocultural turn (Johnson, 2006) that the field of language teacher education has taken thus resonates with our position as teachers and teacher educators for the reasons we described above. In undertaking the research for this book, we used theoretical and analytical lenses derived from the sociocultural perspective.

## Freeman and Johnson's Tripartite Teacher Knowledge Base Framework

The sociocultural turn is a recognition that teachers' expertise evolves from comprehensive sources and that their knowledge is situated. This position is exemplified by Freeman and Johnson's (1998) tripartite framework, which situates the teacher knowledge base in the nexus of (a) the teachers' experiences as learners; (b) the nature of schools and schooling; and (c) the nature of language teaching. This lens allowed us to understand the significance of the data within the context of the lived experiences of the Chinese English language teachers we interviewed and worked with.

The notion of "teachers as learners" focuses on how teachers' prior knowledge, beliefs, and training inform their current instructional practices. It also focuses on teachers as learners of teaching instead of as learners of language, a positive change in a profession that in the past has equated learning a language to learning how to teach it and that regarded teachers as mere "conduits" (Freeman & Johnson 1998, p. 407) for student learning rather than active, thinking individuals with a complex set of factors, influences, and processes that impact their learning.

Teachers' learning experiences are foundational in the ways they eventually teach. Kennedy (1990, cited in Richards & Lockhart, 1994) aptly points out that by the time American students complete their undergraduate work, they have been in classrooms and have observed teaching and teachers for at least 3,060 days, while in comparison most master's level teaching preparation programs take up only 75 days in total. Consequently, the time prospective teachers have spent as learners is probably qualitatively as well as quantitatively more influential on their classroom practices when they assume the job than the formal training they have received. Given this influence, the challenge in the field is to provide time and opportunities for teachers to critically examine what they have learned from being students themselves and the way they were taught.

Both synchronic and diachronic experiences in schools and communities influence how teachers' learning unfolds over time (Freeman & Johnson, 1998). As integral members of their communities, teachers understand not just visible aspects of physical and sociocultural settings but also deeply embedded elements such as underlying values and hidden curricula that are maintained over time. Inherent in this part of the framework are teachers' understanding of and ability to negotiate power, authority, and even what constitutes knowledge and expertise in the environments in which they work (Lytle & Cochran-Smith, 1992). This domain underscores that context is "more than geographical and concrete location ... [as it also] include[s] the sociocultural and sociopolitical contexts, that is, the values and ideologies that inform the policies, practices, and interactions that shape teachers' work" (Sharkey, 2004, p. 282).

The third domain of the framework is predicated on teachers' understanding of their own learners and their learning processes, which, however, cannot "be separated from the teacher as a learner and from the contexts in which teaching is done" (Freeman & Johnson, 1998, p. 410). In this domain, teachers' knowledge is constructed in the context of use and intimately connected to the teacher as the knower. This knowledge not only has relevance to the teacher's immediate situation but is part of the information gathering process that helps the teacher theorize about teaching on a more general scale. From this perspective, teaching and learning are intertwined and inform each other. When teachers see "teaching as learning and learning as teaching" (Branscombe, Goswami, & Schwartz, 1992, cited in Cochran-Smith & Lytle, 1999, p. 281), they see their classrooms as more than a place for application but as a place for growth (Freeman, 2009).

Freeman and Johnson's (1998) framework reflects the notion of teachers' knowledge as "knowledge of practice" (Cochran-Smith & Lytle, 1999, p. 272), in which the positioning of "inquiry as stance" (p. 288) is central. It involves the perspective that inquiry is intertwined with teaching practice and teacher learning. This stance takes the discussion of what teachers know and what their expertise is beyond the following dichotomies:

- *Formal/disciplinary knowledge and experiential knowledge*: Teachers not only draw from disciplinary knowledge (such as second language acquisition [SLA] theory and research) gained in such formal settings as college or professional development programs. They also draw from "a wide range of experiences and their whole intellectual histories in and out of schools" (Cochran-Smith & Lytle, 1999, p. 275). In this regard, teacher expertise is not only the accumulation of provided knowledge but more importantly also the generation of new knowledge and the transformation of existing knowledge. In the same vein, discussion is taken beyond the dichotomy of disciplinary content (such as SLA) versus pedagogical content knowledge, a blend of teaching and content knowledge (Shulman, 1987), and centers on their inseparability as they shape teacher knowledge (see McEwan & Bull, 1991). There is also greater interest in engaging teachers in analyzing and reflecting upon how their "classroom practice, their learning and professional lives and the socio-cultural contexts in which they work" (Freeman & Johnson, 1998) inform their teaching rather than mulling over how to apply a fixed body of disciplinary knowledge in their classrooms.
- *Teaching as practice and teaching as praxis*: Because the relevance of teaching lies in its connections to society at large, there is a dialectical relationship between teaching as manifested in practical action and teaching as a means of advocacy through reflection and taking action to make a difference in society. Teachers undertake both daily. Being informed by the cultures of their communities, schools, and classrooms, teachers' knowledge provides them with the means to question, critique, and take action on issues of equity and social change at the grassroots level through their teaching.
- *Novice and expert teachers*: Knowledge is socially constructed and arises out of teachers' participation and collaboration with peers and others in professional and social milieus. The complexities and uncertainties in daily classroom activities as well as the profession require teachers to constantly frame

and reframe their work at all levels of experience and across their professional life spans. In order to do this, new and experienced teachers have to work together in communities, to "pose problems, identify discrepancies between theory and practice, challenge common routines, draw on the work of others for generative frameworks, and attempt to make visible much of that which is taken for granted in teaching and learning" (Cochran-Smith & Lytle, 1999, p. 293). This kind of intellectual work goes beyond expert–novice distinctions as teachers become involved in inquiry that is not time-bound or based on discrete and unchanging information.

Freeman and Johnson's tripartite teacher knowledge base framework and its convergence with Cochran-Smith and Lytle's conceptualization of knowledge-in-practice underscore the interpretative epistemological stance of teacher knowledge research that investigates what teachers already know and can do and how they make sense of their teaching in their contexts (Johnson, 2009, p. 9). Instead of pursuing "findings" to describe or predict what the teachers should know and do, the goal of research that takes this perspective is to help teachers in "understanding, articulating, and ultimately altering [their] practice and social relationships in order to bring about fundamental change in classrooms, schools, districts, programs and professional organizations" (Cochran-Smith & Lytle, 1999, p. 279). This has been a fundamental focus in our research on Western-trained Chinese English language teachers.

## Activity Theory

The sociocultural perspective not only enabled us to situate teachers' knowledge development but also allowed us to witness teachers' learning (Johnson & Golombek, 2003) and development as well as to draw out their voices as they took ownership of their classroom instruction. For this purpose we chose Engeström's (1987, 1999) representation of activity theory, a second generation extension of the Vygotskyian sociocultural perspective, as our second analytical framework.

Activity theory maps the social influences and relationships involved in networks of human activity, namely the broader network of social, cultural, and historical macrostructures that shape the activity (Johnson, 2009, p. 77). Thus, as Johnson points out, the actions of individuals are not discrete instances but rather are part of a holistic activity system. In this regard, actions mediate and are mediated by relationships with others and by physical and symbolic cultural artifacts within the activity system. Lantolf and Thorne (2006) point out that heterogeneity and multiple voices can lead to conflict and resistance as well as to collaboration and cooperation. Through it all, individuals continue to initiate actions to bring about the most desired outcomes because they are motivated by the need to transform, innovate, and change.

Engeström's (1999) structure of human activity systems provides a cohesive model that brings together the components of activity theory. In this model, the *subject* refers to an individual or groups of individuals taking an action oriented toward an *object*, in order to achieve a desired *outcome*. The object is defined as the problem space or the target toward which the action is directed. *Instruments* are the symbolic or material artifacts (e.g., language or high stakes tests) that mediate the action through their use. *Rules* refer to the guiding principles regulating the actions and interactions in the *community* within which they occur. *Division of labor* takes account of the different roles and responsibilities of the community members in an activity system (Engeström, 1999). Thus one half of the model describes how the undertaking of an action is mediated by artifacts while the other half provides a framework that "brings together local human activity and the larger social-cultural-historical structures" (Lantolf & Thorne, 2006, p. 222). The *outcomes* result from the interactions of the two.

As researchers, we were helped by activity theory to investigate the Western-trained Chinese English language teachers' progression through a series of experiences and contexts that influenced their teaching beliefs and classroom practices, specifically in terms of the communicative language teaching (CLT) approach that is influential in teaching a second language. By focusing on the unique interplay of the contextual variables, cultural tools, and various activities, activity theory also provided us with a lens through which to see how the teachers took ownership of English-language instruction.

In our version of the activity theory model (see chapter 7, Figure 7.1), Western-trained Chinese English language teachers constitute the *subject*. The *object* of the activity comprises the CLT principles they appropriate. The *mediating tools* are the conceptual and practical means teachers use to achieve their goals. *Rules* refer to both implicit and explicit principles influencing the process of teaching and learning. Chinese English language teachers and students make up the *community*. The *division of labor* considers how tasks are divided among teachers, students, administrators, and others. The desired outcome is how effectively these teachers "glocalize" or localize CLT according to the needs of their students and their local contexts (glocalization is discussed below).

The details and complexities of initiating and taking ownership of instructional actions cannot be sufficiently explained by collecting decontextualized numerical data, but can only be captured effectively through a holistic description. Activity theory provided us with a means to analyze and describe these actions in such a way.

## Glocalization

The term *glocalization*, popularized by sociologist Robertson in the 1990s, emphasizes that the globalization of a product is more likely to succeed when the product or service is adapted specifically to each locality or culture it is marketed in. Using activity theory, we found the term useful to describe how the Western-trained Chinese teachers in our study took ownership of their English language teaching when they returned home. Robertson describes glocalization as "the simultaneity, the co-presence of both universalizing and particularizing tendencies" (1997, p. 4). Friedman (1999) defines it as "the ability of a culture, when it encounters other strong cultures, to absorb influences that naturally fit into and can enrich that culture, to resist those things that are truly alien, and to compartmentalize those things that, while different, can nevertheless be enjoyed and celebrated as different" (p. 29). Ross and Lou (2005) point out that "glocalization implies a search beyond the contributions and downsides of globalization in order to conceptualize a world of greater balance between the potentially empowering trends of global communication and the concrete challenges faced by local communities" (p. 229). All these definitions indicate the interplay between global reach and local specificities.

The field of language teaching has also developed its own conceptualization of glocalization. One reason is disillusionment in non-Western settings with Western-based teaching approaches that have limited utility in contexts other than those in which they originated. According to Canagarajah (2005), whose edited book *Reclaiming the Local in Language Policy and Practice* features in-depth discussion of prioritizing the local amidst the global, there are two kinds of responses to globalization in the field. The first is the argument that certain knowledge and practices are universally relevant and can be applied in all places. These homogeneous codes, discourses, and communicative practices, though emanating from the West, are assumed to be standard, so their orientations and biases are widely disseminated under the name of globalization. This position, Canagarajah points out, ignores the equal or greater power of local knowledge in the globalizing process. The second response is that globalization can empower the local through voicing it to the world. However, this phenomenon is being countered by globalization catalysts such as computer-mediated and English-dominated means of communication, which are making it difficult to assert the place of the local and indigenous languages in globalization. Hence, in both responses, Canagarajah asserts, the local is "getting short-changed by the social processes and intellectual discourses of contemporary globalization" (p. xiv).

On the other hand, Canagarajah's (2005) concept of "the local," akin to glocalization, takes greater account of local knowledge and respects its value and validity. He further points out that because knowledge is generated from the "ground-up through social practice in everyday life" (p. 4), the local has major relevance. The concept of localization in language teaching also shows up in Shin's (2006, p. 150) interpretation of "indigenous epistemology" in her work on the colonial legacy and its extension into the classroom where English as a foreign language is being taught. According to Shin, postcolonial language pedagogy, influenced by indigenous epistemology, always questions established and external assumptions and prioritizes local knowledge, and it never provides a one-size-fits-all teaching method. It is important to note, as Canagarajah does, that localization does not mean that the local has a subsidiary or secondary status but rather that it is a radical reexamination of "our disciplines to orientate language, identity, knowledge, and social relations from a totally different perspective" (2005, p. xiv).

To sum up, glocalization encourages a strategic negotiation between the global and the local, leading to diversified and balanced knowledge construction. In a similar way, localization not only involves "deconstructing dominant and established knowledge to understand its local shaping" but also encourages "reconstructing local knowledge for contemporary needs" (Canagarajah, 2005, p. 14). In our research into the experiences of Western-trained Chinese English language teachers, we found their efforts along these lines both courageous and, most of all, creative.

# 3

# HITS AND MISSES

## Shifting Positions in Professional Development of Native and Nonnative English-Speaking Teachers

*When the winds of change blow, some build walls, others build windmills.*

Chinese students who travel abroad to pursue a master's or doctoral degree in teaching English as a second language most frequently go to English-speaking "inner circle countries" (Kachru, 1990), Australia, Canada, New Zealand, the United Kingdom, and the United States, where English is the native language of the majority of the population. For example, there are 157,558 Chinese students attending U.S. colleges and universities comprising 22% of all international students in the United States (Open Doors, 2011). In this book, we focus our interest on Chinese students who have returned home from their tertiary education in English-speaking countries as college-level English teachers. Based on a 2001 study commissioned by the Chinese Ministry of Education (CMoE) that involved English teachers in 354 Chinese universities (Wang, 2011), it seems that these students were formerly in-service teachers in China and part of the estimated 7% of Chinese teachers who have been educated overseas.

## Professional Development of English Language Teachers

We use the term *professional development* to refer to individuals' participation in language teacher education programs either to prepare themselves for or to further their careers as language teachers. These programs can be characterized by the types of knowledge that they are designed to help students acquire. As a microcosm of teacher education as a whole (Crandall, 2000), language teacher education reflects Cochran-Smith and Lytle's (1999, p. 24) distinction among three types of knowledge, which they refer to as "images"; namely, "knowledge-for-practice," "knowledge-in-practice," and "knowledge-of-practice." Knowledge-for-practice refers to formal knowledge and theory generated by university-based researchers to be applied to classroom teaching. Knowledge-in-practice, on the other hand, is grounded in the accumulated experiences of expert teachers, including curriculum decision making, classroom interactions, and other day-to-day practices. These two images of knowledge represent the common distinction between formal and practical knowledge, both of which are to be acquired through study, observation, and reflection. In knowledge-of-practice, however, Cochran-Smith and Lytle blur the distinction between formal and practical knowledge by asserting that teachers are the sources of their own expertise who not only are informed by and transform knowledge but also generate new knowledge. In this ideation, teachers' knowledge is the outcome of their inquiry into their own classrooms and their interrogation and interpretation of "knowledge and theory produced by others" (p. 24). In this regard, Cochran-Smith and Lytle (1999) point out that teachers generate and construct their local knowledge of practice by living their practice; that is, by theorizing it and by connecting it to the social, cultural, political, and intellectual contexts in which they work.

Cochran-Smith and Lytle's (1999) notion of images of teacher learning and knowledge resonates with Wallace's (1991) description of three major models of language teacher education programs for both preservice and in-service teachers: (a) the theory-to-practice model, whereby teachers acquire expert-generated information and apply it to their settings; (b) the apprenticeship model, whereby they learn by observing their mentors; and (c) the reflective model, whereby they take a close and inward look at their own practices in order to evaluate and revise them in ways that correspond to their experiences and settings. Crandall (2000), who included Wallace's description in her review of language teacher models, also saw it as corresponding to that of Donald Freeman's (1991, 1996) analysis of how the view of language teaching has evolved from teaching as thinking (a cognitive model emphasizing theories, strategies, and procedures that teachers learn and apply), to teaching as doing (a behavioral model that emphasizes skills and construes teaching as a craft), to teaching as knowing (an interpretivist model that takes into account why teachers teach as they do in specific contexts, with a focus on helping them to reflect upon their teaching, to interpret theory, and develop skills most useful in their own settings). The last view of language teaching recognizes that teachers are originators of knowledge and not simply consumers or replicators of knowledge. With this recognition also comes acknowledgment of teacher development as a lifelong process of growth that involves autonomous and introspective learning as well as collaboration and social engagement with others (Crandall, 2000).

In tandem with evolving views of language teaching, Freeman (2009) writes of the expansion of second-language teacher education over the years (see Freeman, 2009, Figure 4) along the dimensions of *substance, engagement,* and *outcome* or *influence*. Changes along these dimensions translate into efforts undertaken at different levels and degrees of implementation to increase the relevance of programs in particular and teacher professional development in general. As we briefly mentioned in chapter 2, Freeman refers to *substance* as the content teachers are supposed to learn and how they are to learn it; *engagement* refers to the ways in which professional learning and teacher identity are to unfold over both the short and the long term; and finally, *outcome* or *influence* is seen as gauging the effects of teacher education programs on the development of teacher knowledge and expertise. Freeman points to substance as the axis on which the scope of language teacher education programs turns, from a focus on content as knowledge and skills to involvement of teachers in developing their socioprofessional identity as members of their profession and community. The intersecting axes of engagement and outcome/influence show that movement of the scope of the programs from imitating and recalling to generating knowledge affects not only their students' learning but also teachers' own learning and professional development.

Freeman's expanding gyre is useful for visualizing the design of language teacher education programs and ways to reform them. Sector A in the gyre reflects the conventional designs of programs that focus on replication of knowledge and skills encountered in lectures, short courses, and microteaching. Sector B, in contrast, points to apprenticeship designs that involve immersion in school contexts and learning from mentors. Sector C emphasizes social participation through planned and orchestrated (rather than ad hoc and incidental) efforts to engage teachers in collaboration and learning with others. As illustrations of such activities, Freeman provides examples such as peer-teaching, team-based assignments, and feedback groups.

The evolution indicated in the models discussed above affirms that, as suggested in previous chapters, language teacher education and professional development are experiencing a sociocultural turn. Johnson (2006) defines this turn as a change from a positivistic epistemological stance to one in which learning is viewed as a social process and "not the straightforward appropriation of skills or knowledge from the outside in" (p. 238). Learning is viewed as a process of understanding and knowing mediated by individuals' engagement in social activities.

The extent to which these changing views of teacher expertise and practice impact the design of professional development programs for language teachers is yet unfolding. Despite challenges such as national or state policies that prioritize testing for content knowledge as the main determinant of teacher qualification (e.g., Indiana's Rules for Educator Preparation and Accountability II [REPA II]), the sociocultural perspective is clearly evident in the increasing inclusion of social critical theories (see chapter 2) in language teacher education programs in the United States and many other countries. As Johnson (2006) points out, these theories embed language classrooms, teaching approaches, and interactions within the broader context of social and political relations (Pennycook, 1999, p. 331), and lead to critiquing the ways in which the questions of power and inequality come into play at different levels, in the classroom, institutionally, and in the larger social realm. Typical issues that sustain the theories, Pennycook points out, continue to be those of class, race, and gender, and, of late, sexuality, ethnicity, postcolonialism, and representations of Otherness. The theories and the issues to which they relate stress the critical situatedness of teachers' expertise and knowledge of their profession. From this perspective, professional development programs cannot achieve their goals unless they incorporate teachers' identities, their participation in and understanding of their workplaces, and the intellectual, cultural, social, and political positioning afforded by their contexts and communities.

## Professional Development and Nonnative English-Speaking Teachers (NNESTs)

Increasingly, the topic of professional development programs for NNESTs in inner-circle English-speaking countries (Australia, Canada, New Zealand, United Kingdom, and United States), including their issues and needed changes to the programs, has become the focus of critiques. Of note, in 1998, George Braine of the Chinese University of Hong Kong established the first ever Teachers of English to Speakers of Other Languages (TESOL) Nonnative Speaker Caucus, specifically to give voice to NNESTs in the flagship organization for English language teachers. The conversations featuring these voices have resulted in shifting perspectives on these programs' infrastructures as well as their educational salience for NNESTs.

One of the center points of the conversations is the criticism that language teacher education programs in inner-circle countries do not adequately meet the needs of students who are international nonnative English-speaking teachers. D. Liu (1998) points out that "[I]n spite of their different backgrounds and needs, these students are usually given the same training as their native-speaker peers" (p. 3). He argued that the main reason for this neglect is ethnocentrism in the TESOL field, particularly seen in program offerings. Based on their analysis of 194 graduate TESOL program descriptions and course titles in U.S. universities, Govardhan, Nayar, and Sheorey (1999) point out that no one program "is quintessentially geared toward preparing ESL/EFL teachers for teaching abroad" (p. 122). Kamhi-Stein (2000) reiterates the point when she says that there is currently no single template that matches curricula with the specific needs of nonnative speakers seeking professional development through TESOL programs at the graduate level.

Western-based TESOL programs have also been criticized for their continuing emphasis on second language acquisition (SLA) theories as their central content, viewed as stripped of contextual connections and therefore irrelevant to the daily experiences of teachers. A related criticism is that instructors' academic knowledge of SLA theories is often not combined with pedagogical knowledge or practical experience. From the perspective of international NNESTs, SLA theories are based primarily on cognitive research relating to first language (L1) acquisition in inner-circle countries (Liu, 1998), leaving out the vast number of learners who are acquiring English in other settings and at different stages in their lives (Sridhar, 1994, cited in D. Liu, 1998). Lo (2005) also stresses that there can be resistance from NNESTs when they encounter mismatches between SLA theories and their own learning and teaching experiences. This mistrust in the applicability of the theories is often justified when teachers have difficulty making sense of them once they have returned to their home countries and are working in the field. Nevertheless, as Lo's study demonstrates, what is called for is not the removal of those theories from language teacher education but rather the inclusion of guidance to problematize and interrogate them in light of what teachers know of themselves as learners, of the sociocultural contexts in which they work, and of the actual learning and teaching in their classrooms.

Another issue related to NNESTs' professional development is language proficiency. Many have called for professional development to include English-language improvement classes as part of their offerings for NNESTs (e.g., Cullen, 1994; Kamhi-Stein, 2000; Lee, 2004; Lim, 2011; D. L. Liu, 1999; Shin, 2008). Such structured opportunities for NNESTs to improve their proficiency are thought to be a critically needed element in professional development programs in part because a major reason why teachers study in an English-speaking country is to sharpen language skills and gain teaching confidence. A related issue is the nature of proficiency itself and whether nativelike speaking proficiency remains the desired goal in an era of globalization whereby English speakers communicate not just with native speakers of inner-circle countries but also with nonnative speakers of multiple English varieties (Englishes) in any part of the world. Llurda (2004), citing Alptekin (2002) and Kachru (1992), argues that all the stakeholders involved (e.g., professional development programs, teacher educators, NNESTs) should move away from idealized native speaker norms in both language and culture (Alptekin, 2002, p. 60) toward a concept of English-language communicative competence that reflects "the reality of the uses and users of English" (Kachru, 1992, p. 362). This shift in perspective calls for nothing less than an overhaul in the way professional development programs in the West are designed.

Identity is also an issue in NNESTs' professional development, specifically as it functions negatively to deny access to internships and instructorships; for example, in intensive English programs (IEPs). Adherence to the outdated notion of native speaker status as the premiere qualification for teaching shuts NNESTs out of opportunities to gain experience and legitimacy as English language teachers. Despite abundant acknowledgment in the literature of their qualifications and special strengths, few NNESTs are employed as teaching assistants in IEP programs, which provide fertile training grounds, particularly at the college level (Mahboob, Uhrig, Hartford, & Newman, 2001). This neglect ignores the seismic shifts in the research on NNESTs' identity. Such research exposes the "native speaker fallacy" (Phillipson, 1992) and debunks the perception that native speakers (NESTs) by default are superior teachers of their mother tongue. Non-native speakers may have complementary abilities and, at times, even the upper hand in teaching it. As second language learners themselves, they have insight into what it takes to learn a language other than their own. Cook (1999) points out that this insight provides them with not just empathy but also insiders' understanding of language learning that can inform effective teaching, a fact not lost on Norton Peirce (1995) who challenges the inadequacy of SLA theories to incorporate language learners in the language teaching and learning context. Second, identity research has prompted NNESTs and NESTs alike to reenvision the former's image and role. In a world that overvalues NESTs (Bernat, 2008), such research helps NNESTs overcome the "imposter syndrome" (Llurda, 2005) associated with their feelings of inadequacy, inauthenticity, self-doubt, and low self-esteem. Furthermore, research such as that by Pavlenko (2003) legitimized a third space for NNESTs to view themselves as competent L2 users rather than "failed native speakers" of English (p. 251). Identity theorizing has also been established in the field and has had a similar positive impact on NNESTs' identity. For example, Brutt-Griffler and Samimy (1999) developed conceptual tools to overcome the discourses that prescribe, label, and confine NNESTs' identities and thus devalue their roles and capacities to powerless and disempowering positions. Given the vast amount of research of NNESTs' teacher identity in the field, it is time for employers in Western institutions who are responsible for a majority of NNESTs' teacher education to revisit the research and reconsider their decisions as to whom they should employ.

Another issue is what has been called the "methodological dogmatism" (Reid, 1995, p. 3) of Western-based methods, particularly those labeled "communicative" (D. Liu, 1998). Being viewed as a Holy Grail, they appear in virtually every reform movement. Those who question them are usually stigmatized as "traditional" or "backward" (Kubota, 1998, p. 407), labels often applied to those who struggle to reconcile the demands and expectations of these methods with the vastly different learning traditions, cultural expectations, and policies in their own teaching contexts. Prabhu (1990) challenges this dogmatism by encouraging language teachers to put an end to the search for the "best method" and instead develop their own "sense of plausibility" (p. 161), by which, instead of distinguishing good and bad methods, teachers analyze their teaching according to whether "it is active, alive, or operational enough to create a sense of involvement for both the teacher and the student" (p. 173). Although this process is more complex and uncertain, it is greatly preferable to a quixotic search for an ideal method that guarantees good teaching. Such a search, Prabhu asserts, can often lead to mechanized teaching and overly routinized classrooms.

Kumaravadivelu (2006a), in his declaration of the "death of method," implies that instead of looking Westward, NNESTs should search for professional education and development that facilitates pre- and in-service teachers drawing on local rather than imported knowledge and going beyond the concept of method to understand language teachers as "self-directing, self-determining, and self-motivating" (p. 223) individuals whose own stories inform how they enact their various educational roles. In this "postmethod" era, Kumaravadivelu, like Prabhu (1990), also calls for an end to teaching models in language teacher education programs regardless of whether they are (a) language-centered methods (e.g., audiolingual), (b) student-centered methods (e.g., communicative language teaching), or (c) learning-centered methods (e.g., natural approach). All are flawed in their own ways as evidenced by "ambiguous usage and application, exaggerated claims by proponents and the gradual erosion of their utilitarian value" (p. 162). Above all, Kumaravadivelu points out that teachers' local knowledge has long been ignored where the concept of "method" is concerned in the professional development of language teachers:

> We forget that people have been learning and teaching foreign languages long before modern methods arrived on the scene. Teachers and teacher educators in periphery communities such as in South Asia, Southeast Asia, South America, and elsewhere have a tremendous amount of local knowledge sedimented through years and years of practical experience. But still, all the established methods are based on the theoretical insights derived almost exclusively from a Western knowledge base.
>
> *(p. 165)*

Kumaravadivelu's (2006a) alternative to method is defined by the pedagogic parameters of particularity, practicality, and possibility. The parameters call for language teaching programs to focus professional development on teachers' awareness of contextual particularities, connections between theory and practice, and sociopolitical consciousness.

Pennycook (1989) cautions that rather than being neutral entities, all methods are political and have specific agendas. This discussion is particularly relevant to international NNESTs and their professional development because knowledge of Western methods has traditionally defined their expertise. Pennycook is suggesting that by incorporating these methods, the teachers themselves are being defined in the process. Pennycook argues here that methods and their knowledge bases represent the interests of certain individuals or groups who seek to place teachers in specified roles with specified responsibilities and thus define their successes and failures as teachers. In this way, the methods have, in essence, "diminished rather than enhanced our understanding of language teaching" (p. 597) because of the limited and prescribed lens they impose on how teachers and teaching are to be viewed.

The positions emerging from the issues concerning language teacher education programs discussed above point to the prioritization of teacher insider and local knowledge as well as the necessity of situated rather than standardized professional development for both NESTs and NNESTs. These positions converge with the sociocultural movement currently in place in the profession of teaching English as a second/foreign language. In light of this convergence, Johnson (2006) identifies four challenges facing the profession: (a) moving away from the dichotomy of theory versus practice to praxis, by which teachers have opportunities to "make sense" of the theories in their professional lives and in settings in which they work (p. 240); (b) accepting the legitimacy of teachers' knowledge and the multiple forms of teachers' ways of knowing instead of looking for generalized principles of effective teaching (p. 242); (c) "redrawing the boundaries of professional development" to include teachers' classrooms and their social participation in professional networks and informal settings (p. 243); and (d) recognizing the need for "located teacher education," requiring the incorporation of the social, political, economic, and cultural histories of the contexts in which teachers teach (p. 245) into any teacher professional development program.

To take one fundamental point from all the complexities discussed above: given that 80% of English teachers around the world are nonnative speakers of English, a major paradigm shift away from externally prescribed methods to locally crafted improvisations drawing on both academic and experiential resources is irreversibly underway. The conversations around this point will only increase. We hope the book can be a generative force that continues to move the conversations along as the wind would move a windmill to generate new thoughts and ideas.

# 4

# EVOLVING LANDSCAPES

## Chinese Positions on Communicative Language Teaching (CLT)

*Be not afraid of changing slowly; be afraid only of standing still.*

Chinese scholars and practitioners have had varied positions on communicative language teaching (CLT) that are shaped by both local and global histories and events. The positions may be broadly categorized as acceptance, resistance, and adaptation of CLT in China. They are discussed below following a discussion of the highlights of the CLT approach.

### Main Goals and Principles of CLT

Communicative language teaching originated from dissatisfaction with the audiolingual and grammar-translation methods in foreign language teaching and learning. It started in the late 1970s and developed widely in the early 1980s. Since then it has been perceived, rightly or wrongly, as a universally accepted model of language instruction (Richards, 2005). The central core of CLT, according to Kumaravadivelu (2006b), is the fostering of competence in social interactions identified as "communicative competence" (p. 60). Originally conceived by Dell Hymes in 1972, the notion of communicative competence was further developed by Canale and Swain (1980) to go beyond linguistic competence to include sociolinguistic, discourse, strategic, and grammatical competencies. Sociolinguistic competence consists of learners' ability to use the language appropriately in social situations; discourse competence refers to their ability to combine grammar and meaning to express themselves in new, different, and fluent ways; strategic competence is the use of verbal and nonverbal strategies to cope with challenges of communication; and grammatical competence is the accurate and effective use of the features and rules of language. Jacobs and Farrell (2003) went on to identify eight defining elements underlying CLT principles, namely: (a) learner autonomy; (b) the social nature of learning; (c) curricular integration of English into other subjects; (d) focus on meaning through content-based language instruction; (e) diversity and students' individual differences in learning; (f) language as a means to promote critical and creative thinking; (g) multiple and authentic assessments; and (h) teachers as colearners in the classroom. Overall, the purpose remains the development of adequate activities and opportunities for students to use their English for real communication and authentic purposes.

## CLT Classroom Highlights

Three defining features of CLT classroom instruction have emerged from the elements discussed above, namely, (a) student-centeredness, (b) flexible teacher roles, and (c) purposeful and scaffolded activities that promote communicative engagement.

### Student-Centeredness

In a student-centered classroom, students' readiness for autonomy is acknowledged. In addition, they are seen not simply as learners but as managers of their learning. Thus, they are not regarded as passive knowledge receivers; instead, they are encouraged to negotiate meaning in their interactions with peers as well as teachers. Littlewood (1981) notes, "it is the learners themselves who are responsible for conducting the interaction to its conclusion" (p. 18). For instance, in pair work and group work, the learners are given the freedom to choose their partners and activities; to design and select tasks; and to find ways to express their individual opinions in creative and multiple ways. Ideally, it is the learners who decide what and how they want to learn. In this regard, different voices, different needs, different learning styles, and different experiences of the learners are taken into account in CLT.

### Flexible Teachers' Roles

CLT provides teachers with the latitude to play multiple roles such as instructors, cocommunicators, needs analysts, advisers, negotiators, colearners, and activity designers (Ellis, 2006; Kumaravadivelu, 1993; Littlewood, 1981; Swain, 1985). Their roles in the classroom are decentered from "sages on the stage" or dominant authority figures in the classroom to "guides on the side" as facilitators who use their own language abilities, what they know about students, and open-ended and information-gap activities they design to promote communication in the classroom. CLT thus provides teachers with the flexibility to assume multiple roles and to decide what and how to teach with CLT principles in mind.

A less frequently mentioned but major role in CLT is that of responsive teachers who develop or assemble materials that are aligned with the expressed interests of their students and fit their needs as learners. Consequently, teachers often develop a repository of "realia" or materials from authentic sources to use in the classroom in ways that allow students to not only be exposed to but also participate in using language in context.

### Purposeful and Scaffolded Activities for Communicative Engagement

All activities are geared toward situations in which genuine communication can take place. To that end, there are several features that distinguish CLT activities from those in other approaches. One is that there is a balance between "focus on forms" and "focus on meanings" in communicative activities. The former refers to a focus on grammatical accuracy while the latter emphasizes effectiveness in getting messages across. In a summary of the characteristics of communicative activities, Richards (2005) pointed out that the role of grammatical accuracy should be recognized for its contribution to communicative competence so both inductive and deductive learning of grammar should be emphasized in the activities. This comes as a surprise to many as CLT is often stereotyped as being adverse to grammar instruction.

Meaningful engagement in real communication can be achieved only if students "can participate not only with their 'learning' selves, but with their whole selves" (Medgyes, 1986, p. 109). In order to achieve this goal, Kumaravadivelu (1993) offered macrostrategies that scaffold engagement to include utilization of learning opportunities that are created by learners, using them as cultural informants, and activating the intuitive heuristics of learners as they seek to convey their message, a process not only of learning but also of self-discovery of their own effective communication strategies. Even when a mandated textbook is used, CLT principles provide scaffolding guidance on different ways for teachers to engage students in communicative interactions by organizing the content so as to tap into their curiosity and personal knowledge. For example, open-ended but scaffolded activities that engage students in using language to reach their own communicative goals are mainstays of communicative classroom activities. They can include activities that are task-, theme-, project-, and problem-based. In this way, students are provided with pathways to communicate and, most importantly, to use their time in the classroom in a purposeful and meaningful manner.

Littlewood (1981) points out that in CLT, balancing between language forms and meanings is a matter of degree that depends on contextual factors, not prescribed formulas. Hence, there is a flexible continuum between linguistic form-oriented activities and meaning-oriented activities as well as between accuracy and fluency. For example, if the focus is on meaning on a certain day, teachers can decide not to correct students' errors in order to encourage their efforts to express themselves. However, teachers can help and support students in their efforts to get their meaning across. On the other hand, teachers may decide to correct certain errors immediately if they are significant enough to prevent students from being understood (Ellis, 2006).

The above discussions point to the fact that there is much to recommend CLT. However, it has its critics. As Prabhu (1990) points out, all approaches are flawed, and there is no one best method. These criticisms are part of the discussions in the next section on CLT in China.

## Communicative Language Teaching in China

CLT's position in China is reflective of the major changes the country has been experiencing. In 1955, 6 years after the founding of the People's Republic of China and the establishing of a policy that mandated Russian as the only foreign language to be taught, Chinese officials realized that excluding English from the school curriculum would be detrimental to the country's efforts to extend its markets throughout the world. Accordingly, the Chinese Ministry of Education (CMoE) announced that English teaching should be reinstated in secondary schools. Consequently, in 1962, English became part of the entrance examination for colleges and universities. This was a period during which the English language and the Western cultures in which it was a native tongue were of great interest. However, the Cultural Revolution put a temporary end to the English language revival, banning it for the duration of the revolution, from 1966 to 1976.

Interest in English was reignited in China with drastic changes in 1978, spearheaded by Deng Xiaoping's Four Modernization and Open Door policies. Since then, English language teaching has been vigorous, and English has been reinstated as a compulsory subject in junior and senior secondary schools and at the tertiary level. In 2001, English instruction was introduced in the third grade in urban elementary schools, and there are significant efforts currently to extend it to rural elementary schools. English has thus been gaining popularity and a prominent position in Chinese education. In addition, despite many changes in the recent history of Chinese English language teaching, the basic motivation for the Chinese to learn English has remained constant, namely, "as a necessary tool which can facilitate access to modern scientific and technological advances, and secondarily as a vehicle to promote commerce and understanding between the People's Republic of China and countries where English is a major language" (Cowan, Light, Mathews, & Tucker, 1979, p. 466).

However, according to Ouyang (2000), the primarily utilitarian nature of these motivations may not be accommodated by CLT, which nevertheless has become the centerpiece of educational reform, replacing traditional methods and resulting in much frustration and resistance. To understand this opposition, it is necessary to highlight the differences between the two approaches.

Traditional methods are based on the principles of Confucianism, by which teachers are to "propagate doctrine, impart professional knowledge and resolve doubts" (Han, 1993, p. 56). Students, for their part, are supposed to receive and assimilate the teachers' words as well as follow their instruction using prescribed and centralized textbooks. The English teacher is at the center of instruction and spends most of the class time explaining English vocabulary, syntax, and grammatical features in the native tongue (i.e., Mandarin), while students repeat and memorize them with the help of textbooks. Reading aloud is a popular in-class reinforcement activity, and it is very common to find a student standing up next to his or her table or in front of the class to lead the read-alouds after the class completes each unit in a textbook. These activities are accommodated by the grammar-translation and audiolingual methods that CLT was conceived to displace.

Being "situated in a much larger context of social and educational change in contemporary China" (p. 397), which now prioritizes quality education through creativity and individuality (Zhong, 1999), English language teaching reform, which is now led by CLT advocates, challenges the effectiveness of traditional methods to meet the country's urgent need for large numbers of English proficient individuals for a wide variety of functions. Lin (2002) points out that the college students who have studied at least 8 years of English using the traditional methods are unable to communicate effectively with native speakers, even on a basic level, disadvantaging the Chinese in a world increasingly dominated by English. In a *China Daily* article, He (2000) expressed this sentiment most succinctly when she attributed this failure to students being spoon fed information by teachers who were doing most of the talking from the front of the class.

Realizing the shortcomings of traditional methods, Xiaoju Li, a Chinese teacher of English, began to write and teach from a set of "Communicative" textbooks. In 1984, the publication of Li's article "In Defense of the Communicative Approach" in the *ELT Journal* marked the shift from the traditional grammar-translation and audiolingual methods to communicative language teaching of English as a foreign language in China. However, it was not until 1992 that CLT gained prestige throughout the country. The State Education Development Commission (SEDC), as the representative of the Chinese central government and the official authority for making educational policy, introduced a new teaching syllabus with the stated goal of using English for communication. By the mid-1990s, teachers were required to teach communicatively; students were encouraged to use English for communication; and textbooks were designed with communicative activities. However, in tandem with the macrodrive to implement CLT as part of overall educational reform, among educators three identifiable positions regarding the approach emerged.

## Three Positions on CLT in China

### *Acceptance of CLT as Progress*

As mentioned above, the traditional English language teaching method in China, a combination of the grammar-translation and audiolingual methods, is characterized by explicit and systematic instruction in grammar, extensive analysis of linguistic details and patterns, emphasis on translation, and strong reliance on memorization and repetition. Both teachers and learners have realized that what they teach and learn is an analytical knowledge of the language in its written form but students have poor ability to speak or understand it in spoken form, even after many years of English language studies (Lin, 2002, p. 8). Thus, it is apparent even to the general public that the traditional methods fail to help teachers and students develop the ability to use English for real communication in a country where there is the largest population of learners of English in the world.

Consequently, Chinese educators and officials have very high expectations of CLT to develop both teachers' and learners' communicative competence in English. Accordingly, its implementation has been mandated by the Chinese State Education Development Commission (SEDC), the official authority for issuing Chinese educational policy. In this top-down way, the government has established CLT as a progressive educational reform that will benefit Chinese society. For example, Li (1984), one of the first proponents of CLT in China, argued that CLT had already improved English language teaching in China, and later Zhou (2001), after observing about 30 English classes and interviewing teachers and students, stressed that CLT allows for interesting class activities, less pressure to memorize, more active student participation, and more listening and speaking opportunities. Liao (2004) claimed that, despite the challenges, "the application of CLT will bring about a positive effect on English teaching and learning" (p. 272). In his case study of a Chinese secondary school teacher, he found that the teacher could overcome such situational constraints as large class size and limited resources to implement CLT successfully. He asserted that "if teachers are aware of situational constraints, any difficulties can be overcome" (p. 271).

In keeping with Liao's claim that "CLT is best for China" (p. 270), its incorporation has been vigorously executed. G. Hu (2002) points out that "resources have been expended on revamping curricula for various levels of education, updating English syllabuses to include principles and practices advocated by CLT, producing communication-oriented English textbooks, developing skill-oriented examinations, and upgrading teachers' knowledge of new language-learning theories and pedagogies" (p. 94).

## Resistance to CLT as an Imposition

Although CLT ideology and practice have been highly influential in the English language teaching world since the early 1990s, they have also incurred a great deal of criticism. The main thrust of the criticism is that in their claim of universal applicability, CLT proponents neglect contextual and local factors. Kumaravadivelu (2006b) concluded that in many settings CLT "is out of sync with local linguistic, educational, social, cultural, and political exigencies" (p. 64).

In the case of CLT in China, the three elements (student-centeredness, flexible teacher roles, and communicative activities) mentioned above as defining CLT pose monumental challenges. One of the most often cited obstacles to taking CLT's student-centered approach is the large number of students (anywhere from 48 to 70 or more students) in a Chinese classroom (Hui, 1997). Proponents of CLT might suggest that large classes simply call for students to assume some of the responsibility for teaching and learning with the teacher acting as coach. The Chinese criticism is that only the top students can benefit from this type of approach while the rest are at a loss as to what to do without adequate and appropriate attention from the teacher. Additionally, even the top students are not always sufficiently proficient to undertake student-centered activities, much less to lead the learning of others (Qing, 2004).

Student-centeredness is also interpreted as promoting individualism and thus challenging the deep-rooted ideals of collectivism (Yan, 2000) and rules of interpersonal civility in China. Indeed, one rationale for adopting CLT has been to produce more assertive and creative communicators in China. But this abrupt reversal of tradition is perceived as promoting student dominance in discussions and aggressive debating while the teacher's authority is sidelined. This negative view of the personal arrogance and denial of the contribution of others associated with individualism is represented by an old Chinese saying, "the bird taking the lead is usually the one shot first" (qiāng dǎ chū tóu niǎo).

An underlying principle of CLT is the flexible roles of teachers, and that in itself represents a related cultural challenge. Teachers have traditionally been the unquestioned authority figures in Chinese classrooms. One practical reason is the centrality of highly structured standardized gatekeeper tests in Chinese education, which remains in an odd-couple relationship with CLT. As the direct agents of their students' success on these tests, teachers are obligated to help students get high grades (Ng & Tang, 1997), a situation that prevails in tertiary as well as secondary education. All Chinese college students are required to pass the College English Test (CET-4) after 2 years of English classes. At both levels, these high-stakes assessments force teachers to take a teacher-centered approach in instruction to ensure that all content to be tested is covered.

Cultural reasons for resistance to flexible teacher roles have also been cited. First, in traditional Chinese education, the teacher's primary responsibility is the transmission of knowledge that students need as a foundation for further learning (G. Hu, 2002). This results in students' heavy reliance on their teachers (Qing, 2004), in return for which they have absolute respect and trust in their teachers' capability and knowledge. This deferential relationship is in direct contrast with the teacher's role as a colearner and facilitator in CLT, where teachers and students share and deconstruct their uncertainties together in the process of learning and constructing new knowledge. The coequal relationship implied in those roles suggests that teachers should assume self-deprecating positions so as to encourage students to participate in sharing knowledge (Hai, Qiang, & Wolff, 2004) while keeping activities light-hearted to encourage engagement (Hu, 2002). These changed positions compromise the teacher–student power differential that has been the foundation of teachers' intellectual and social positions and thus, causes them to "lose face" (Yan, 2000).

Additionally, CLT's focus on spontaneous interaction and engagement presents a challenge to the Chinese tradition of reverence for knowledge, commitment to serious study, and painstaking efforts to learn (G. Hu, 2002). In this regard, it is not surprising that Burnaby and Sun (1989) reported that teachers who taught communicative rather than analytic skills had low status in the Chinese school system. As another Chinese saying goes, "strict teachers produce outstanding students" (*yán* shī chū **gāo** tú), and CLT can be viewed as turning all important educational values on their heads by diminishing the status and therefore the effectiveness of the teacher in the classroom.

Another reason why there is resistance to CLT in China is the perceived high cost, both mental and financial, of teacher preparation. First, CLT communicative activities place a high demand on Chinese teachers' oral skills in English and cultural knowledge of countries in which English is a native language (Qing, 2004). But there are limited resources available for teachers to acquire what they feel is an adequate level of oral proficiency. For example, Wang (2011) reported that 84% of college-level Chinese English teachers had no overseas experiences, 83% had never attended an overseas conference, and about 40% had not attended any domestic conferences. Consequently, teachers often feel their English proficiency is not sufficient for them to teach effectively through CLT. Also they often deem CLT as geared more to the needs of students who are about to study overseas than those of other students (Burnaby & Sun, 1989). Given their limited experience and training, many teachers feel prepared mainly to help students to read academically in English, which has been considered as the primary goal of teaching English especially at the college level (Fei, 2004).

Additionally, in order for communicative activities to be engaging and relevant, CLT teachers usually need to develop their own materials and syllabi so as to address students' expressed needs and specific interests, and this is a divergence from the norm of a prescribed curriculum and mandated texts. These responsibilities require additional time and effort on the part of teachers who are likely to be juggling multiple teaching and private tutoring jobs both in and outside school to supplement their income. To manage it all, Hui (1997) pointed out that "what they do frequently, instead, is lecture to students using the readily available printed texts and language points, which makes their teaching easy and safe but proves to be non-communicative and ineffective" (p. 2). She also points out that photocopy facilities are not always accessible and authentic resources in the library and elsewhere are scarce and not always available to all teachers.

Uneven and limited distribution of resources was also cited as a CLT challenge. Based on a study of 439 secondary school graduates from 25 provinces and municipalities of China, G. Hu (2003) pointed out that schools in both developed and rural regions could not fully implement CLT because of a shortage of financial resources to support curriculum reform and teacher training. The situation, of course, is especially bad in the rural areas, where, besides lower funding, schools suffer the loss of qualified English teachers to more prosperous areas. Consequently, although CLT implementation is a mandate, 70% of secondary schools in rural areas are unable to follow through with it.

With growing awareness of the problems associated with the top-down imposition of CLT on Chinese teachers, a primary criticism has been its neglect of the local context, a very important aspect of any language pedagogy (Bax, 2003a, 2003b; Harmer, 2003). Bax (2003a) sharply argued that "CLT is now having a negative effect and needs to be replaced as our main focus" (p. 278). He stressed further that the time has come to replace the current CLT approach as the central paradigm in China with a more contextualized pedagogy, to which we would add, a more culturally responsive pedagogy as well.

## Adaptation of CLT as a Pragmatic Consideration

There is increasing interest in adapting CLT to the demands and cultures of Chinese EFL teaching and learning. Adaptation is seen as a pragmatic choice for a country that has arrived as a key player on the global stage. As the currently ascendant global language, English is a necessary accessory for this role. For example, there is an expectation that those going into the Chinese labor force should have fluent English oral skills, both in speaking and comprehension (Sun & Cheng, 2002). Accordingly, so as not to lose the benefits of CLT's emphasis on these skills, the Chinese government has taken the lead in overcoming resistance and supporting the effective adaptation of CLT.

This process was begun with the goal embedded in the Chinese Ministry of Education's (CMoE) 2003 English language standards for curriculum reforms to "transcend subject centeredness" (Zhu, 2007, p. 225). Another step was to direct teachers to work on students' speaking and writing skills as well as the intensive reading, memorization, repetition, vocabulary acquisition, and translation that are still predominant across the nine levels of standards. In this way, the standards are gradually being modified to support productive and communicative uses of English (Lin, 2002). At the ninth and most advanced level, particularly in public high schools that emphasize foreign language studies, students are expected to be able not only to understand lectures, discussions, debates, reports, and foreign broadcasts but also to express views of domestic and international concerns, to be interviewed in English, to clarify misunderstandings verbally and in writing, to translate, to express their feelings, and even to understand and engage in humor in English. Somewhat more complex are adaptations in the English standards that attempt to balance the communicative use of English and Chinese values. The standards advocate English language proficiency development by knowing the larger world and at the same time by becoming "familiar with local situations, traditions and social development" (Zhu, 2007, p. 225). Thus, the standards position the use of English to face outward and inward at the same time. Outwardly, English should enable students to increase their knowledge of other countries' geography, traditions, lifestyles, art, literature, behaviors, and values. However, more importantly to the CMoE, English is also promoted as a means for students to communicate these aspects of Chinese culture to the world, a process by which they develop patriotism through self-reflexivity as they gain a deeper understanding and appreciation for their own Chinese culture and language.

A third move by the CMoE to integrate the communicative approach into the standards is its call for teachers not to rely solely on textbooks but also to use CLT project- and task-based activities to engage students in authentic, hands-on problem solving. Collaboration in pairs and groups, which provides ample opportunities for students not only to learn from each other but also to experience "a collective sense of honor and achievement," well illustrates the blending of the old and the new.

These principles of adaptation have been reinforced by the State Education Development Commission (SEDC), which has issued a statement encouraging teachers to use eclectic methods that combine the innovative elements of CLT with traditional Chinese methods (Liao, 2000). This statement is backed up with calls for further measures, such as reforming English tests to include language skills for communication, for example, listening to dialogues, and answering questions; raising the quality of English-teacher training in CLT; and improving teachers' English proficiency and communicative abilities. Also the communicative aim of teaching and learning English is frequently reinforced through official government statements and pronouncements.

Another important adaptation is to treat the traditional approach/CLT relationship not as dichotomous but as complementary. For example, Sun and Cheng (2002) described how a private college in Guangzhou developed an English language program that accommodated both traditional and CLT approaches. The program consisted of two parts: instruction by Chinese teachers using traditional methodologies such as grammar-translation and text explanation for 5 or 6 hours a week, and oral English instruction by expatriate teachers focusing on "speaking and listening, with communicative competence at its core" (Sun & Cheng, 2002, p. 77) for 2 hours a week. At a public governmental school ranked as the top high school in Beijing, we observed a similar arrangement but with a focus on content area subjects. In the morning, students received instruction in the content areas from their Chinese teachers, and in the afternoon, expatriate content area teachers taught the same subjects in English. The aim of the program was for expatriate teachers to introduce English in a meaningfully communicative manner. Although such an arrangement makes a long day for the students, it is a pragmatic approach that draws on the strengths and experiences of both Chinese and expatriate teachers.

Other calls for juxtaposition of Chinese and CLT approaches can be heard. Interest in CLT is evident in published research, which generally also calls for adaptation. For example, in an investigation of 30 Chinese university students' perceptions of communicative and noncommunicative activities in the EFL classroom, Rao (2002) found that most of the students favored a combination of communicative and direct teaching activities. She argued that Chinese EFL teaching should align the communicative approach with traditional teaching approaches, that is, "combine the 'new' with the 'old'" (p. 85). In particular, the misconception that grammar had no role in CLT, a major reason for students' disapproval of the approach, needed to be corrected. As she pointed out, the communicative approach and the Chinese traditional grammar-translation method are not mutually exclusive (Ellis, 2006; Rao, 1996). Rao (1996) suggested that it is possible to maintain a balance between form and meaning-focused teaching, provided grammar is treated as a tool or resource, instead of the end goal of instruction. To successfully combine these approaches, "the teacher must be organized and skillful in integrating the communicative components with the components of the grammar translation method" (Rao, 1996, p. 469).

Another advocate of melding long-standing features of Confucius-based learning with the new culture of communicative language learning, Shih (1999) argued that instead of doing away with traditional practices, teachers can use them to address communicative ends. For example, while traditionally English texts are read aloud meticulously "as a way of learning new words and grammatical structures" and the purpose of writing in English is to develop skill in "producing correct language" (p. 20), these reading and writing practices can be applied to communicative ends by providing literacy tasks that involve real life purposes and development of new perspectives on issues of true interest to students.

Jin and Cortazzi (2006) proposed a "participation-based" model of language learning in the classroom through communication and interaction. They described traditional English learning in China as exemplified by the saying, "an army crossing a lone-log bridge" (p. 10), which implies that while many start out early to learn English and strive continuously, only a few will make it across the narrow bridge of examinations. This approach thus requires discipline and concentrated attention of students in classes in which they listen and observe carefully so as to learn and remember content, the accuracy of which is further reinforced by teacher-mediated and book-based interactions. The model Jin and Cortazzi proposed expands language learning beyond the linguistic level to a multidimensional construct that includes cognitive, creative, affective, sociocultural, and metacognitive engagement. For example, in the creative dimension, instead of repeating scripted dialogues, students are encouraged to take risks with language and to express themselves in new ways. Thus, participation remains learning-focused and purposeful but at the same time it allows for student-centeredness through autonomy and experimentation.

The adaptation of CLT in the Chinese context, and in particular, the task-based language teaching approach within it, according to Carless (2008), also requires a flexible balance between use of the mother tongue (MT) and of the target language (TL). As previously mentioned, task-based teaching involves students working to achieve non-pre-determined and usually nonlinguistic outcomes using information that is provided by the teacher. In undertaking the tasks, students use the target language purposefully to develop the products of the given tasks. However, "[t]he more absorbing the task, the greater is the students' use of the MT" (Carless, 2008, p. 235). In this context, the MT can be a useful and positive resource as a humanistic and student-centered strategy important in task-based language teaching (TBLT) and CLT, but it is important for teachers to be able to distinguish between activities in which it is an appropriate tool, such as those involving linguistic or conceptual analysis, and those in which the TL should be used such as in communicative undertakings.

In short, pragmatism and the principle of the "golden mean" drive efforts to adapt CLT to the Chinese EFL classroom. These efforts are defined by an ideological stance which recognizes culturally embedded diversity and rejects the notion of universally appropriate ways of teaching and learning English (G. Hu, 2002). Liao (2004, p. 40) sums it all up by saying that "a method is not equally suited to all contexts, and different methods suit different teachers and students in different contexts" (p. 270).

In the next chapter, we will see the preparation that Chinese English language teachers undergo to study overseas. The process involves the teachers being able to demonstrate that they can communicate effectively in English. Just like CLT in China, the process has gone through an evolutionary process that has made it increasingly competitive and complicated.

# 5

# THE MIDDLE KINGDOM AND BEYOND

## The Pathways to Chinese English Language Teachers' Journeys Overseas

*It is better to travel ten thousand miles than to read ten thousand books.*

*Zhōng guó,* or "the Middle Kingdom," is the Mandarin word for China. Semantically, it also denotes the historical centrality of the Chinese emperor's seat in the known world, and by extension, the importance of the highest level of authority. Although not at the same level of grandiosity but at the highest level of educational importance, two documents prescribe all educational policies in contemporary China, including those governing students or visiting scholars going abroad: the 12th 5-year plan for National Economic and Social Development (NESD) (2011–2015) (China Direct, 2011) and the Outline of the National Long-Term and Short-Term Education Reform and Development Plan (2010–2020) ("Outline," 2010). The documents originated from the State Council (*guó wù yuàn*), an official body synonymous with the Central People's Government since 1954 and the chief administrative authority of the People's Republic of China. Together, the documents provide new goals for Chinese education and emphasize the importance of teacher education, in particular the need to increase the number of teachers and to improve the instructional efficiency of primary and secondary schools.

Toward this end, at the 17th National People's Congress (October 15–21, 2012), the annual meeting of the highest officials for the government of the People's Republic of China, an announcement was made that in the coming 5 years, the country will "give priority to education and turn China into a country rich in human resources," and "cultivate large numbers of talented people who have international perspectives, who understand international ways, who are able to engage in global affairs and compete at the international stage"

("Outline," 2010, pp. 5, 34). All these decrees bode well for Chinese English language teachers who include overseas education in their future plans.

## Scholarship Programs and Chinese English Language Teachers

By offering scholarships, both local and national governments consolidate their influence and retain their connection with teachers. This is the case for Chinese English language teachers, as government-sponsored scholarships are the most accessible, although there are numerous funding programs from other sources including from private donors, corporations, and foundations. Table 5.1 provides a comparison of the specificities and the conditions set by various sponsoring agencies for their scholars.

**TABLE 5.1** Comparisons across Scholarship Programs (CSC, 2012b)

| Program Name | Sponsors | Time Coverage | Special Conditions | Application Schedule |
|---|---|---|---|---|
| CSC visiting scholar / post-doctorate program | Chinese Scholarship Council | 3–12 months | | All year round; more programs are offered in March (Each year, changes and updates are announced on their website). |
| Building High-level University PhD program★ | | 36–48 months | Under 35, specific universities and majors | |
| PhD Cooperative Program / National Major Project | | 36–48 months | Under 35 211 / 985★★★ Universities | |
| SC Masters Degree | | Based on particular contracts | 211 / 985 Universities | |
| Undergraduate Exchange Programs★★ | | 12 months | 211 / 985 Universities | |
| Western Areas Visiting Scholar Programs | Chinese Scholarship Council & home universities | 3–12 months | | December |
| Young Backbone Teacher programs | | 3–12 months | 211 / 985 Universities | March and September |
| Local government scholarships | Financial Bureau of local provinces | Advanced scholar: 3 months / Ordinary scholar: 12 months | | October to November |

| Program Name | Sponsors | Time Coverage | Special Conditions | Application Schedule |
|---|---|---|---|---|
| International Cooperation Programs | Chinese Scholarship Council & Host University | Based on contracts | | Based on contracts |
| Foreign Foundation programs | Foreign foundations, (e.g. Ford Foundation, Fulbright) departments or institutes | Depends on different programs, usually no more than three years. | Programs can determine students from which universities should attend | Varying times |
| Special Talents Program (International Regional Studies /High-level Foreign Language Proficiency / Art /Music) | Chinese Scholarship Council | Undergraduates: 6–12 months; Visiting scholars: 3–12 months Master / PhD degrees: 6–24 months Post-doctorate: 3–12 months | | March |

\*    Self-financed students can also apply.

\*\*    Available programs are announced each January, usually limited to certain foreign universities.

\*\*\*    Highest ranking universities in the 211 or 985 list of schools, for example, Peking, Tsinghua, Beijing Normal, Shanghai Jiao Tong, and Zhejiang universities, etc.

Although there are no policies specifically aimed at supporting Chinese English language teachers and teacher educators to go overseas, these two groups of professionals comprise the majority who go abroad under Chinese government sponsorship, especially as visiting scholars. (For an example of a popular government scholarship program, see the Chinese Scholarship Council [CSC] in Table 5.2). The main reason is that English teachers meet the strict official requirement for applicants to have a high proficiency in English. Consequently, any teacher with a bachelor's degree in English may be eligible to go to English-speaking countries without additional requirements. However, teachers who did not major in English must demonstrate their English proficiency; for example, by scoring 80 or above on the Internet version of the Test of English as a Foreign Language (TOEFL); scoring 5.5 or above on the International English Language Testing System (IELTS): or reaching level 5, the highest proficiency level, on the Chinese Ministry of Education's Public English Test System (PETS).

**TABLE 5.2** 2013 CSC Scholarship Plans (CSC, 2012a)

| Programs | Categories | No. of Available Scholarships |
|---|---|---|
| Building High-level University Administrator Programs | PhD | 2500 |
| | PhD in dual/cooperative programs | 3500 |
| Visiting Scholar Programs | Advanced Scholars / Visiting Scholars / Post-Doctorates | 2500 |
| Young "Backbone" Teachers (Teacher Leaders) Programs | | 3000 |
| Undergraduate Exchange Programs | 211 / 985 universities | 2000 |
| Special Talents Program | Art / Music | 200 |
| Western Visiting Scholar / Local Cooperative Programs | | 1500 |
| Administration Department Cooperative Programs | | 500 |
| Foreign Cooperation Programs | Student exchanges | 950 |
| International Regional Studies / High-level Foreign Language Programs | | 1050 |
| Master's Degree (New) | | 300 |

The prevalence in the number of English language teacher applicants is exemplified by those from Yunnan Normal University (YNU) who applied for scholarships to go overseas. Over the past 10 years, two thirds of teachers going abroad have been English teachers. However, of late, they are facing stiff competition from teachers who work in other fields. For example, in 2011, of 10 YNU candidates who were eligible to apply for the local government scholarship, only four were English language teachers. Teachers in subject areas other than English have begun to obtain high English test results which make them eligible as well for the government scholarships. English and therefore the desirability of going abroad are also becoming more pervasive in Chinese higher education. Finally, the most important reason of all is the government's promise of employment to all its sponsored graduates and scholars upon their return. All of these reasons trump the anxiety that applicants may have regarding the obligations and commitment to serve the government upon their return home. In this regard, the centrality of the government in the lives of individuals is sustained. As we will explain later, however, there has been increasing difficulty in identifying nongovernment support sources.

## The Processes of Application and Acceptance

With few exceptions, for both local/provincial government sponsorships and national sponsorship programs, the intricate application process involves tight control and accountability measures. Along the way, applicants must obtain approval from multiple officials including Communist Party representatives and the process ends with the applicants reporting all of their activities to the respective Chinese offices while they are overseas.

The application process (see Table 5.3) begins with an application form available online, on which numerous signatures are required. When the application has been accepted, the applicant attends an oral interview by local experts (*běn dì zhuān jiā*), who assess both English language proficiency and the significance of the proposed research. Once the applicants are successful in gaining sponsorship, they must make a deposit of 20,000 yuan (between approximately U.S.$3,500 and $4,000) to the sponsoring agency. They will also be sent for mandatory training on foreign regulations (e.g., visa applications) and tips for how to live and study abroad. Upon completion of the training, a certificate is issued, without which government agencies will not help the applicants with further steps even if they have been awarded scholarships. Successful applicants also have to sign a "coming back home" agreement by which they pledge to fully reimburse the government's funding of their studies if they fail to return. Once all the processes are completed, the applicants then will have to seek out their own overseas programs and faculty who will agree to host them. In some cases, professors will request interviews with the applicants before agreeing to host the students.

Finally, once students are abroad, they will have to regularly report their performance (every 6 months or so) to the Chinese agency that is sponsoring them. They also have to submit their travel itineraries so as to keep the agency abreast of their travel plans in the foreign country. Following is a depiction of the application and acceptance process of one type of award, Local Government Visiting Scholar Sponsorships. Applicants seeking CSC sponsorship for PhD degree programs should be accepted into CSC-approved doctoral programs before they apply for scholarships. Being successfully accepted into one of these programs guarantees that applicants will be supported by the CSC for 36 to 48 months to complete their studies, with a possibility of an extension. Alternatively, the applicants can choose an unendorsed university and major(s) of their choice, but the CSC will not extend support beyond the originally specified period, at which point applicants must support themselves. Nevertheless, once applicants are accepted into a doctoral program overseas, CSC scholarship is almost assured, provided that the applicants abide by processes and steps outlined by the government.

## Hurdles and Challenges

There are many hurdles in the process, and much perseverance is needed for them to be successfully cleared. As the Chinese saying goes, "perseverance can whittle a steel pillar down to a thin needle." One of the main challenges is the

**TABLE 5.3** Processes of Application for and Acceptance of Local Government Visiting Scholar Sponsorships

| Scholarship Application | Foreign/Host Program Application | Acceptance of Offer |
|---|---|---|
| 1. Application form: Application forms are usually downloaded from International Affairs Office website. Signatures are required on the form from several agencies including from the International Affairs Office, Human Resource Department of the home university, CPC Party Administration Office of the home university, and local Educational Administration Office (usually the Education Bureau). <br> 2. Oral defense: Local experts decide who can get the scholarship based on the English proficiency and importance of the research the candidates propose. | 1. Visiting Scholar application: Apply into the "visiting scholar" program in the host university. <br> 2. Interview: This is sometimes required by the professor who will host the student. <br> 3. Offer acceptance letter: Submit host university invitation letter and other documents for visa application. <br> 4. Document submission: Submit documents required by the host university. | 1. International affairs training: Local International Affairs Office will administer the training for each candidate who received the scholarship. It is a compulsory process which results in a certificate and a financial support letter signed by the Education Bureau. <br> 2. "Going abroad" approval letters: Apply for the "*Approval Letter of Official Staff Going Abroad for Private Affairs*" from CPC Office of home university; from CPC Bureau of local province; from International Affairs Bureau of the local province. <br> 3. Guarantee deposit: Usually 20 thousand yuan. <br> 4. Receipt & processing of the Scholarship: Apply for the "*Approval Letter of Large Amount of Money Exchange for Official Affairs*" from Financial Bureau of local province; money transfer from official account of university to Bank of China; exchange money at the Bank of China <br> 5. Ticket booking: Hand in guarantee deposit and photocopy of passport and visa to International Office of Educational Bureau to book the ticket. <br> 6. Contract: Sign the *Coming Back Contract* with local Educational Bureau and notorize the contract. <br> 7. Information upon arrival at the host university: Register personal information at the website of Chinese Embassy of host country. <br> 8. Report regularly activities, travel plans to the Embassy. |

complexity and lengthiness of the application process. It can take as long as 6 months to a year or more for the applicants to fill in forms, visit many offices for signatures and permissions, and sit through interviews, all of which must be accomplished within the limited period, usually 3 years, before the scholarship offer expires. For example, a teacher who applies for a scholarship in 2010 and obtains it in 2011 will usually not be able to take care of all details and leave for overseas until 2012, the last year of the scholarship offer. Moreover, although the local and national government share similar application and acceptance processes, other agencies may not. The different process for each agency causes additional frustration for applicants.

Another hurdle is a time limitation of a different kind. Though there are many types of scholarships each year, the government policy is that teachers can only apply for one local government or national scholarship every 5 years. If they fail in one application, they may have to wait for another 5 years, which may mean a 10-year waiting period. This prolonged delay is problematic, especially when changes in life circumstances affect eligibility. For example, agencies give preference to applicants who are under 35, and the wait-time between applications can mean that an applicant ages out of eligibility. The length of time between when scholarships are offered and applicants actually depart is also a significant problem because the amounts offered may not be sufficient for economic realities 2 or 3 years later, even though the amounts allocated vary in accordance with the locations where the teachers wish to pursue their studies. As a consequence, applicants may eventually find themselves needing to supplement their income while abroad.

A government policy that stands in the way of many is the preference given to applicants from elite universities targeted for significant government funding to develop China and improve the country's international reputation. Although there are many applicants from other institutions, sponsoring agencies look to sponsor those who are from "211/985" universities; that is, high-ranked universities such as Peking, Tsinghua, Beijing Normal, Shanghai Jiao Tong, and Zhejiang universities. This policy puts applicants from lesser known universities at a disadvantage.

In the past decade, fewer and fewer foreign institutions and foundations have included China as one of the countries that receive their scholarships owing to the rapid expansion of the economic development of the country. This change of policy has especially limited scholarship programs, especially for secondary school teachers. For example, in cooperation with the University of Reading, England, the CSC has one subprogram for secondary school teachers within the Western Areas Visiting Scholar Programs. However, the program accepts only 36 teachers per year. Although teachers can seek professional development from international training companies such as the HYDE International Company, without any kind of sponsorship these training programs are unaffordable for most.

Nevertheless, there are an increasing number of scholars who are invited to go abroad, for example, to teach Chinese. The Chinese government and the collaborating agencies in foreign countries split the scholars' salaries between them. A prominent example of this joint venture initiated by the Chinese government is the Confucius Institute programs that are situated in many places abroad. However, for English language teachers, this governmental program is not always available to them because, despite being native speakers, Chinese-language teaching is not their subject area. This is unfortunate because these teachers, as we will see in later chapters, are among the best cultural brokers and are an essential force in leading China's internationalization efforts.

## The "Call" of the West

We began our research into Western-trained Chinese English language teachers by utilizing interview data that was made public by the International Office of one of the universities where our teachers worked. The information was derived from 14 English language teachers, who were interviewed in depth regarding the countries they wanted to study in; the reasons why going abroad was important for them; and their hopes and dreams of what they would achieve by going abroad. The information also included the sacrifices teachers anticipated they would experience.

The table below illustrates the countries of choice. Not surprisingly, the United States, Australia, the United Kingdom, and Canada ranked high. However, Singapore is increasingly emerging as a country of interest and attests to the current Chinese view of Singapore as a model of its future when ability in English will play a critical role in making China a "halfway house between authoritarianism and liberal democracy" (Harcher, 2012, para 18).

Experiencing a different culture (35.7%) appears to be the most important reason for teachers to go abroad (see Table 5.5 below). To learn about a previously unknown culture or to be immersed in novel cultural experiences were

**TABLE 5.4** Chinese ELTs' Countries of Choice

| Countries | N | % | Rank |
|---|---|---|---|
| USA | 14 | 100 | 1 |
| Australia | 10 | 71.4 | 2 |
| UK | 10 | 71.4 | 2 |
| Canada | 8 | 57.1 | 4 |
| Singapore | 7 | 50 | 5 |
| France | 2 | 14.3 | 6 |
| India | 2 | 14.3 | 6 |
| Japan | 1 | 7.1 | 8 |

**TABLE 5.5** Reasons for Going Overseas

| Group | Expand academic experience | | Experience different cultures | | Improve academic ability for career / EdD / PhD | | Cooperate with foreign scholars, meet job needs | | Learn from host professors | | Fulfill dream | | Broaden views of world | | Create opportunity for family members | |
|---|---|---|---|---|---|---|---|---|---|---|---|---|---|---|---|---|
| | N | % | N | % | N | % | N | % | N | % | N | % | N | % | N | % |
| Teachers | 4 | 28.4 | 5 | 35.7 | 4 | 28.4 | 2 | 14.2 | 5 | 35.7 | 2 | 14.2 | 3 | 21.3 | 1 | 7.1 |

Reasons

reasons given as the primary goal for the Chinese English language teachers, and to one teacher, it was an important part of professional development:

> I am interested in the American culture, especially because English is my major in China. So to visit and experience the "native life" there plays a big role in my lifelong plan.

The two top professional incentives were improving the teachers' academic abilities and expanding their academic experiences, both at 28.4% of responses. As the comment below illustrates, going abroad for cultural reasons (35.7%) was closely intertwined with professional goals:

> As an English teacher and professor, I consider it very important for me to visit and study in English speaking countries to improve my English and gain more knowledge about the people, the culture and the government. As the saying goes, "behind our own mountains, skies or people, there are others we can learn from."

Cooperating with others and developing professional relationships overseas (35.7% and 14.2%) also ranked high in terms of the reasons for going abroad, as is evident in the following statement:

> I want to go abroad because I want to initiate cooperation with foreign scholars in both research and teaching. On the one hand, it can broaden my view and facilitate my academic ability. On the other hand, I want to build up long term cooperation with foreign scholars so as to have more cross-cultural research in the future.

Building relationships is considered an important source of social capital in Chinese society. Having good relationships, especially with influential individuals, will, as the Chinese saying goes, "double the results with half the effort" (*shì bàn gōng bèi*).

There are also personal reasons that motivate English language teachers and professionals (7.1%). For those who are parents, going abroad is a way to create opportunities for their children to obtain a better education, particularly in English-language learning. Some visiting scholars even find ways to get their spouses admitted to the same host university so as to enable their children to remain overseas longer

> I went abroad for three reasons: first, to get a PhD, which is my life dream; second to broaden my life experiences; third, to create an opportunity for my wife and son to go abroad, especially so that my son can learn English.

In some circumstances, the opportunity to go abroad makes it possible for couples to have an additional child, as was reported to us by one of the people surveyed. The "one-child" policy is still in place in China although it is currently being revised so that a couple can have more than one child if the husband and wife each are the only child in their respective families. The implementation of this new policy was not yet fully in place at the time of the writing of this book. Going abroad thus remains a viable option for those seeking to include an addition to their family.

The survey results demonstrated the lure and the possibilities of going overseas. However, as with all things, challenges exist and are the subject of much consternation.

## The Other Side of the Coin: The Sacrifices

There is a Chinese saying that "you cannot have the fish and palm of the bear at the same time," meaning that one cannot have two valuable things at the same time, and one has to make a choice between them (in Chinese tradition, the fish is a metaphor for life and the palm of the bear for justice and refers to occasions when an ultimate sacrifice may be required). More generally it means that one cannot have it all and sacrifices have to be made. The first sacrifice of going overseas may be time away from one's immediate family. Being a part of a culture in which family plays a major role in life makes this is a major sacrifice:

> Going abroad in order to learn more was my dream, but I lost the chance to take care of my parents, which makes me feel guilty.

Choosing the right moment to do the right thing is an important life mantra in China. As evident in information from the survey, choosing between conflicting values was not an easy decision. Time away from China can affect promotional opportunities. For example, pursuing a PhD in China usually takes 3 to 4 years, but it can take as long as 7 years in the United States. That time away can impact job promotions: First, in an academic position, one's rank increases according to the number of years on the job or the expansion of one's institution. If one is away, one will be displaced from the promotional sequence. Second, time away from one's position also reduces the networking opportunities that sustain one's connections and influence that can support one's promotional chances.

Another sacrifice of going abroad is related to the time, often perceived as wasted, that must be allocated to the adjustment period needed by those who return home after a lengthy sojourn abroad. Upon their return, many soon realize that what they learned in foreign countries does not fit well or is not urgently needed in the Chinese context. They then need to invest a lot of time and effort to reconcile the differences in order to find a place and firm footing for themselves professionally as well as personally. This process can be long, painful, and in the eyes of several who responded to the survey, an unnecessary waste of time. Nevertheless, despite the difficulties of returning home after an extended time abroad, many return to the Middle Kingdom to be welcomed home as wizened "sea turtles."

## Returning "Sea Turtles" (*hǎi guī*)

A significant trend of late is the high return rate of scholars sent abroad, representing a return on investment and justifying the increase in the number of people being sent overseas. A statement from the Chinese Ministry of Education (CMoE; 2012), reports that from the beginning of the Open Door Policy in 1978 to 2011, a total of 2,245,100 students pursued their education abroad, of whom 818,400 Chinese students had returned home from overseas, a 36% return rate, whereas in 2011, 186,200 students had returned from 339,700 sent abroad, a return rate of 55% with others presumably continuing their studies. Contrary to popular opinion that a significant number of those who return are government-sponsored students, the majority are privately sponsored. Among the returnees, 9,300 were Chinese Scholarship Council (CSC) scholarship holders, 7,700 were local government or institutional awardees, and 169,200 were students funded from private resources.

Sea turtles are known for their ability to find their way back home even after being far away for a very long time. In the same way, the Chinese government hopes that the lure of the rapidly expanding Chinese marketplace will bring their overseas-trained and highly talented students back home to the embrace of their motherland, the Middle Kingdom, a country that is playing a central and influential role in global dynamics.

# 6

# LIGHT AND HEAT

## The Empowerment, Validation, and Anguish of Having Been Trained Overseas

*When one gains in one area, one loses in another.*

There are over 2 million Chinese English-language teachers (Braine, 2010), of whom many, as described in chapter 5, go overseas for graduate study as a part of a broad, concerted effort to elevate the quality of English-language instruction. When these students return home, they are pioneers in introducing Western-based language teacher training to pre- and in-service teachers whose prior training and experiences are, for the most part, Eastern. Given the challenges these returning educators face, understanding the outcomes of their study abroad is essential, not only for improving their preparation in the West, but also for the benefit of the Chinese government agencies, universities, and other institutions that send them.

To begin to achieve this understanding, the present chapter focuses on information in response to the question of how Chinese English-language teachers' learning experiences in Western countries impact and challenge their teaching in China. We focus in particular on the impact of communicative language teaching (CLT), which has emerged as a preferred if not mandated approach in many Asian countries. We begin with a description of who these teachers were and how they shared their teaching and learning lives with us.

### Lǎoshī: Teachers or People of Old and Deep Wisdom

*Lǎoshī* (Teachers) Fangxue, Meiling, Hongyue, and Lichang (all names in the study are pseudonyms) received graduate training in the United States, Australia, and New Zealand. At the time of the study, they were teaching at the two largest and highest ranked universities in a province in southwest China. Both universities are located in the center of the provincial capital city and are similar in size: approximately 2,500 faculty and staff, and 20,000 full-time undergraduate and graduate students. The first university is a comprehensive university, which prepares its English majors for various English-language related careers, and the other is a teachers' college, which trains English majors for local teaching careers. This pattern of one key comprehensive university and one key teachers' college is typical of Chinese provinces.

The four participants were teaching in different capacities but had several characteristics in common. While Fangxue and Meiling were college English-language teachers, Hongyue and Lichang were teacher educators, and all had received graduate degrees in English as a second language teacher education programs in English-speaking countries. Teacher Fangxue and Teacher Hongyue held doctorates, while Teacher Meiling and Teacher Lichang had earned master's degrees. At the time of the study, all were active in-service teachers who had taught English at the college level for at least 4 years before going abroad, and returned to teach in their original universities after completing their studies. Teacher Fangxue was the only male teacher in the group.

## Information, Reflection, and Insight

For 4 months, we recorded our conversations and interviews with the teachers in Chinese and spent time with them daily in their classrooms. We also reflected together on our conversations with each of them and undertook stimulus recall interviews (Shkedi, 2005) while viewing randomly selected videos of their teaching with them. The teachers also shared with us their teaching materials, including their syllabi, lesson plans, and instructions for assignments. Additionally, they gave us access to the records of the courses they had taken abroad, the annual reports they submitted to their schools, and their publications. Together, we kept daily notes with documentation of and reflections on the research process. Finally, in order to understand and identify the significance of the information we were accumulating, we used the sociocultural lens of Freeman and Johnson's (1998) tripartite framework (see chapter 2). Table 6.2 provides an overview of the multiple sources of the data we accumulated.

## Returning Home to Light and Heat

In response to our question, the teachers shared with us information in terms of knowledge that they came away with from the West and the consequences of that knowledge. Freeman and Johnson's framework enabled us to see that the teachers' knowledge and expertise were situated in the nexus of their experiences with regard to (a) what they had gained as learners, (b) their knowledge of the learning and teaching processes that take place within their own classrooms, and (c) local institutional and cultural circumstances, the interdynamics

**TABLE 6.1** Teachers' Backgrounds

| Teachers | Age and Sex | Number of Years Teaching Before Going Abroad | Years of Studying in West | Western Educational Background | Years of Teaching After Overseas Education |
|---|---|---|---|---|---|
| Teacher Fangxue | 45 male | 11 years | 8 years | PhD in TESOL and Curriculum and Instruction in USA | 2 years |
| Teacher Hongyue | 40 female | 7 years | 6 years | PhD in Education in Australia | 4 years |
| Teacher Mahua | 30 female | 4 years | Two years and a half | MA in Education in USA | 6 years |
| Teacher Lichang | 32 female | 9 years | One year and seven months | MA in TESOL in New Zealand | 2 years |

**TABLE 6.2** Multiple Information Sources

| Data Sources<br><br>Teachers | Classes Observed | Class Observations (videotaped) | Before-Class Interviews (tape-recorded) | After-Class Interviews (tape-recorded) | Post-Observation & Stimulus Recall Interviews (tape-recorded) |
|---|---|---|---|---|---|
| Teacher Mahua | *English for Academic Purpose*[1] (Non-English major graduate students) | 16 hours | 2 hours | 3 hours | 1 hour |
| Teacher LiChang | *College English* for non-English majors (Second-year undergraduate students) | 20 hours | 2 hours | 5 hours | 2 hours |
| Teacher Fangxue | *College English* for non-English majors (First-year undergraduate students) *Curriculum Theory and Practice* (Second-year English-major graduates) | 24 hours | 1.5 hours | 3 hours | 1 hour |
| Teacher HongYue | *Intercultural Communication* (Second-year graduates/ in-service English teachers) | 35 hours | 2 hours | 3 hours | 1.5 hours |

1 All course titles are pseudonyms.

of which required them to situate and problematize their training in terms of these actual contexts.

The framework thus provided us with a means to identify specific aspects of the teachers' knowledge along with its impact. The two were intertwined and presented a complex picture. In particular, Western education empowered teachers' pedagogy and practice but, at the same time, complicated the teachers' lives by providing a comparative lens through which they could critically reflect on its utility in the Chinese context and raise questions about the feasibility of the changes it implied within existing circumstances. In the following section we discuss these complexities and the various aspects of the teachers' knowledge in which they were grounded.

**TABLE 6.3** Impact of Western-Based Language Teacher Training on Four Chinese ELTs

| Freeman & Johnson's Framework | Impact of Western-Based Language Teacher Training | |
|---|---|---|
| Teachers' knowledge of themselves as learners | Western knowledge empowered teachers | • Empowered teachers by helping them to solidify personal outlook, teaching beliefs and principles<br>• Empowered teachers by strengthening their professional position and confidence<br>• Empowered teachers through improved English Language proficiency |
| Teachers' knowledge of classroom teaching & learning | Western knowledge empowered teaching | • Empowered teaching/learning by providing frameworks to enhance course design<br>• Empowered teaching/learning by providing means to enhance teaching tools |
| Teachers' knowledge (comparative) of sociocultural contexts of school and schooling | Western knowledge engendered critical perspectives | • Enabled teachers to interrogate the overall "goodness" of their Western-based training<br>• Enabled teachers to validate the relevancy of local knowledge and practice<br>• Enabled teachers to take ownership of CLT |
| | Western knowledge complicated teaching lives | • Challenged teachers' ability to reconcile teaching to existing school dynamics<br>• Challenged teachers' ability to bring about changes to existing educational infrastructure |

## Western-Based Training Empowered Teachers and Teaching

Although there was diversity in their opinions, all the teachers agreed on the empowering impact of their overseas educational experiences, with which they associated increased professional self-confidence. Not surprisingly, they were well aware of how valuable it was for their professional growth to be immersed in a language and an educational culture quite different from their own, and that it brought about real changes in their teaching. Such awareness is one of the three fundamentals of teaching expertise (Freeman & Johnson, 1998). But while all four articulated the empowering impact of their education, they varied in how they interpreted it. Teacher Lichang focused on professional growth and especially the new confidence she had gained, which would now become the impetus for experimenting with change and trying new practices:

> My professional knowledge was expanded and my teaching methods were also enriched. My confidence was reinforced as an English teacher, really. You know, in the past we were mirrors of our own teachers. That has changed.
>
> *(Teacher Lichang, Interview, May 24, 2009)*

In a later interview, Teacher Lichang speculated further on how she had changed in terms of both understanding and practice, as she now saw her role as providing guidance and support rather than transmitting knowledge:

> What I was very satisfied with was that I was able to use what I learned in the West in my teaching, which made my classroom not traditional. My role is to support and guide students, to help them use resources such as portfolios to understand what they are learning. I am proud that I can continue to proceed with these beliefs and methods to this day, years after I came home.
>
> *(Teacher Lichang, interview, August 7, 2009)*

In a similar way, Teacher Meiling expressed how her Western education moved her to deep reflection on who she was as a teacher, and even more profoundly, how she viewed the relationships between knowledge, education, and being human:

> I always think of "Brookstone" [pseudonym for a U.S. university] as a turning point in my whole life. It is as if a window in my heart has opened. I have a clear mind now on what kind of person I want to become and how I am going to educate my next generation. I ponder over issues on being a human being because this is the foundation of education, and education is not only an issue of knowledge.
>
> *(Teacher Meiling, interview May 22, 2009)*

She also found that her image had changed in the eyes of her students in a way that reflected how they learned:

> My students have high expectations of the teachers who get degrees from overseas. They look up to you and are very curious about overseas learning experience, very curious.... The experience abroad gave me the confidence that I implicitly pass on to students.... They think my teaching methods are new and the teaching is centered on students' thinking. They know I want them to think.
>
> *(Teacher Meiling, interview, May 22, 2009)*

Teacher Hongyue took away the message of learners' autonomy and responsibility for their own learning, a perspective that she thought had strengthened her as a student abroad and would also benefit her students by developing their independence:

> The classes I attended in the West consisted of many international students at different levels of English proficiency. No matter which countries the students came from, the professors taught students according to the criteria they already had. Of course occasionally some professors would show concern about your language struggles but ... they think you should go to ask them if you have questions or cannot understand the class. At this point, I thought that should be the case for graduate students here, too.
>
> *(Teacher Hongyue, interview, July 19, 2009)*

Teacher Hongyue was especially conscious of the control she felt she had over the English-language, something she could gain only by direct experience:

> The study of English I experienced before going overseas was actually a kind of "making a cart behind closed doors." You are using other people's experience, the indirect stuff, to learn, but after going abroad, the experience becomes yours.... Now if I need to speak in English, I just speak. Whatever the topic is, I can talk about it with confidence.
>
> *(Teacher Hongyue, interview, August 19, 2009)*

In addition to empowering them personally, the teachers' Western training enhanced their teaching in concrete ways. The resources they acquired ranged from practical tools for teaching to macroparadigms for course design and improvement. The tools they mentioned included technology, activities such as process writing, and course management tools such as providing students with a syllabus:

> In the past I, like other Chinese teachers, never did that [gave students a syllabus]. Wasn't that true of you too? Chinese teachers' syllabi were written for the administrators, not the students. Now I give a syllabus to

all the students in each of my classes, and I include my name, class time, phone number, e-mail, course objectives. That was the first thing I did after returning from the U.S.

*(Teacher Meiling, interview, May 21, 2009)*

The teachers also reported that their Western training led them to develop new courses or revamp the way they taught existing ones. Of particular note is Teacher Hongyue's decision to take the courageous step of using English as a medium of instruction in her cross-cultural communication course, fully aware of the limitations of her "nonnative English" and her students' struggles to keep up with the course in English. Her overseas training emboldened her to deal with the discomfort of English immersion for both herself and her students and forged ahead despite collegial judgment, which might even become appreciation:

> My colleagues think I am different.... They attribute my differences to Western learning. But I have always been different from a young age. Western learning encouraged my alternative thinking and original ideas. My colleagues may think that I can be foolhardy, but they also acknowledge that I am inventive and brave.
>
> *(Teacher Hongyue, interview August 19, 2009)*

## Western-Based Education Enabled Problematization and Validation of Chinese Ideas

While teachers acquired new resources and found new energy from their Western training, their knowledge of two quite different cultural contexts enabled them to develop a critical lens (Freeman & Johnson, 1998):

> You have to critically use the things you learned in the West. You cannot just grasp all of them and say they are all good. It is like you are saying that everything there is terrific and that the outside way is the best. It was good, and maybe very good on that soil, but that is not so certain when you bring it here for use here [i.e., in China].
>
> *(Teacher Hongyue, interview, August 19, 2009)*

Teachers used this critical lens to interpret and assess the principles and methods of communicative language teaching (CLT) in the Chinese context, most saliently how this approach could be brought into harmony with traditional practices they still highly valued and were unwilling to discard. For example, they resisted the CLT principle of equality in teacher–student interactions as unrealistic given the nature of classroom protocol in any setting. As Teacher Hongyue pointed out:

Teachers are teachers, right? It is impossible for you to establish a totally equal relationship with your students. In the West they cannot achieve that either…. So this authority of the teacher is definite.

*(Teacher Hongyue, interview August 19, 2009)*

For Teacher Meiling, CLT's minimization of teachers' authority could be detrimental for learning, especially if it compromised their ability to point out mistakes straightforwardly:

Teachers' authority should always be there even in communicative activities…. You should be able to criticize students. In the West, if you criticize students…oh, my god, it is impossible. But did you notice that in the West, you have to agree with students even if they were not on track? I think this is completely not right…. You criticize students not because you want to let out your emotional frustrations; you criticize them for their sake…. But in the West whether you are sincere or not in trying to help students, you dare not criticize students. That way, sometimes the boundary of good and bad is not clear. I do not think this works for Chinese people.

*(Teacher Meiling, interview, May 21, 2009)*

In addition to pointing out CLT tenets that did not fit the Chinese context, the teachers also came to the defense of much maligned practices in traditional Chinese language teaching such as memorization and recitation, choral reading, and translation. For Teacher Fangxue, memorization and recitation were valid ways to provide practice in a setting in which there is limited external English-language input:

Rote learning and memorization and recitation are necessary and should definitely be maintained…. Westerners have to use them as well when they are teaching languages here…. Memorization and recitation have their own merits because, you see, in this language learning environment, it is impossible for students to really speak English. Only through this rote learning can they internalize what they learn. Students do not have many opportunities to speak and hear English.

*(Teacher Fangxue, interview, July 19, 2009)*

Teacher Meiling agreed that memorization and recitation were critical to providing useful models of English-language usage:

We do not have an English-language context…. I would never ask my students to memorize without an aim, or just randomly. In my intensive teaching, I would pick well-written sentences or sentences that show common useful features. I would select them deliberately and ask students to memorize them for future use.

*(Teacher Meiling, interview, May 21, 2009)*

The teachers also defended group reading, a common practice in Chinese English-language classrooms that is often viewed critically by Western observers as a form of passive language practice. However, Teacher Lichang saw the practice as a way to lower the level of apprehension for struggling students while creating opportunities for all to participate:

> I do not like asking an individual student to respond because I have been a student before.... If you call their names individually they will not speak even though they want to speak. They dare not speak. If I always ask the active students, other students will feel neglected. So, I deliberately let them answer questions chorally [as a group].
>
> *(Teacher Lichang, interview, June 29, 2009)*

The teachers also agreed that translation was not contradictory to communicative purposes:

> My own understanding of CLT is that translation and real communication are [part of] a process, a continuum; and we cannot regard them as two extremes.
>
> *(Teacher Lichang, interview, June 8, 2009)*

Teacher Hongyue saw translation as consistent with the Western bilingual principle of using students' native language as a stepping stone to learning a second or foreign language:

> I choose to use Chinese to translate whenever I find there is difficulty and problems in comprehension. I considered this as a strength and advantage for me and the students. This is a current practice in bilingualism I learned about abroad.
>
> *(Teacher Hongyue, interview, July 19, 2009)*

In summary, the four teachers reflected critically on what they had learned in their Western training and took ownership to reconstruct it in ways responsive to the specific circumstances of their situations (we discuss the teachers' "localization" of CLT practices extensively in chapter 7).

## Western-Based Education Posed Challenges to the Status Quo

While the four teachers considered their Western education as empowering, the critical perspective it enabled also complicated their lives by making them aware of incompatibilities between what they experienced in the West and their workplace realities in China. In addition to instructional challenges in the classroom, the teachers were also confronted with difficult administrative and collegial issues after returning home.

At the instructional level, the teachers faced several obstacles in implementing CLT. These obstacles included their students' limited exposure to English, which made it a challenge to implement the active, open-ended engagement that CLT requires. Also, the teachers taught large classes that could range from 40 to 70 or more students seated in inflexible rows, necessitating the teacher-centered approach characteristic of lecturing. Such classroom arrangement was compatible with students' and parents' expectations of good teachers as information providers, which ran counter to CLT's emphasis on students as agents of their own learning. Teacher Hongyue explained this issue the following way:

> For our students, if you let them participate in various activities in class, some students will complain that although the teacher's class is fun and interesting, they learn nothing. They feel that the concept of "learning" means that the teacher should tell them that this lesson was about these and those points and the students want the points explained to them.
>
> *(Teacher Hongyue, interview, August 19, 2009)*

Textbooks also posed a challenge because their underlying goals of ensuring uniform instruction and preparing students for national tests were in opposition to the teachers' perceptions of the goals of CLT. Indeed, the importance of these exams in students' educational careers highlights what may be the greatest systemic obstacle to CLT in China. As Teacher Fangxue explained:

> It would be much easier if we did not use the unified textbooks and if we did not need to complete the unified curriculum.... Currently we have to finish at least nine units out of ten and this is a big task. If I just teach them four units, the students will complain that I did not finish the textbook.... All of these materials serve the purpose of Band Four and Band Six College English tests, and they do not have any relation with communicative language teaching.... The unified textbooks and teaching plan affect one's beliefs of good teaching.
>
> *(Teacher Fangxue, interview, August 18, 2009)*

At the administrative level, the teachers' status as Western-trained educators did not always grant them the authority to make changes. For example, Teacher Lichang's efforts to have a say in student assessment met a "brick wall":

> When I asked the administration about the content of the listening test, they said they were not clear. When I asked them about the format of the testing, they told me that I did not need to ask because someone had already looked into that. When I asked them what I could do to help, they asked me to write a test and to turn it in. But they did not let me know what kind of format to work from or what they took from the test I wrote or which elements they chose or anything.
>
> *(Teacher Lichang, interview, June 8, 2009)*

Administrators evaluated teaching on the basis of the teacher's performance, not the students' learning, which virtually mandated teacher-centered methods. Teacher Meiling described her experience with the "Expert Inspection Team," a group of senior professors who came to observe her annually, as follows:

> The Expert Inspection Team came to observe my class and asked me whether I could lecture more. They said I lectured too little.... It was just because I left time for students to think, let them reflect, and ask and answer questions. I responded to the team that the content could be found in both the syllabus and the textbooks. They still thought I was not providing enough content knowledge ... because they still used the traditional criteria to evaluate how I lectured, presented the logic of my arguments, provided a convincing elaboration, and showcased my English expressive ability. These were what they were concerned about.
>
> *(Teacher Meiling, interview, May 21, 2009)*

A similar indifference to new ideas was often forthcoming from colleagues, which led Teacher Lichang to express a sense of dejection:

> When I returned from abroad, I was very active and eager to share with my colleagues. I even made CDs and put them in the office so whoever was interested could view them; but later I found that even if I gave my colleagues the materials in person, they would not read them or said they had no time for that. Actually this was not the case. They felt that the experience they accumulated for many years was enough. Indeed they wondered why I had to impose my ideas on them. I had no way to demonstrate that I was successful.
>
> *(Teacher Lichang, interview, May 24, 2009)*

The saving grace for Teacher Lichang was to focus her energies on students. Despite collegial disdain she was "happy to introduce Western learning to students and to share with them personal experiences of living in a foreign country." In her enthusiasm, she even decided to take on 6 hours of classes in addition to the 8 she was already teaching.

Teacher Lichang's enthusiasm underscored the fact that despite the challenges these Western-trained Chinese English-language teachers faced, their dedication to the profession and especially to their students was unwavering. The joys they found in teaching are captured in Teacher Fangxue's poetic metaphor:

> If we were to be in a flower garden, I would prefer to follow my students, watching them enjoy themselves, and letting them discover the beauty of the world. At the same time, I would feel extremely glad because they would be learning something in a pleasant environment. So, a satisfactory trip or a journey to the garden would always bring two things: great plea-

sure and knowledge about the "wonders".... Very often what we learn from such wonderful experiences will remain in our minds forever.

*(Teacher Fangxue, interview, May 22, 2009)*

## Reflections on Information: Wisdom Is Learned in Different Ways, Reflection Is the Noblest

In contrast with previous studies that emphasize a mismatch between teachers' training abroad and realities at home, our findings demonstrate both positive and negative consequences for these Chinese teachers. They acknowledged that their education abroad posed new challenges but also empowered and enriched them personally and professionally. While their Western training "did not always get it right," as one teacher in the study put it, they were able to make use of their knowledge within the constraints of their situations without either rejecting their overseas education or accepting it in its totality. Instead, they saw it as their responsibility to look for a language pedagogy that combined "global appropriacy with local appropriation" (Kramsch & Sullivan, 1996, p. 199) and so occupied a middle position. In this way, they took an interpretive perspective that, in line with Freeman and Johnson's (1998) tripartite framework, called on their knowledge of themselves as learners, their insider knowledge of the teaching and learning processes in their classrooms, and their knowledge of the sociocultural contexts and infrastructure in which they lived and worked.

The findings also show that the teachers' appreciation of their own culture was reinvigorated when they returned home. They determined that many Chinese traditions and practices were valuable and should be sustained alongside innovations from abroad. These findings concurred with Ha's (2004) and Sullivan's (2000) studies of Western-trained Vietnamese EFL teachers, who felt that their effectiveness increased when they incorporated locally expected behaviors into their teaching.

Their experiences abroad changed the teachers into individuals with unique experiences and expertise. However, they also resulted in the teachers' personal and professional isolation. The teachers' attempts to share knowledge with colleagues were met with refusal and even disdain, despite being in a cultural context in which teacher collaboration is highly prized and is especially encouraged in the public schools through collaborative teacher research groups known as *jiàoyánzǔ*. The experiences of teachers in this study demonstrated that a similar teacher collaborative sensibility does not always make its way up to the college level.

To be fair, collaboration is difficult to achieve in all organizational structures including schools, where the convergence of multiple personalities, values, agendas, and pressures often fosters conflict (Achinstein, 2002). Collaboration is most likely to be successful when organizational and interactional factors that sustain it are in place (D'Amour, 1997). In terms of organization, leaders need to support collaboration through formalized structures such as protocols and procedures. Productive interaction among colleagues requires sufficient mutual trust to share ideas and goals and to rely on each other's knowledge and abilities. Such trust is built over time through repeated instances of positive experiences working together (San Martín-Rodriguez, Beaulieu, D'Amour, & Ferrada-Videla, 2005). Our findings suggest that the leaders and colleagues in the teachers' workplace were not always open to changes or the collaboration that might produce it. Nevertheless, the teachers in this study had not given up, but, as Teacher Hongyue suggested, gaining the recognition and acceptance of others was a work in progress:

> Some would admire or others would envy you. You brought them [col-leagues] something new. You do not have to show it off…. It should be demonstrated through teaching activities over time…. I never told my colleagues directly about it, but I believe they will eventually notice my Western education background.
>
> *(Teacher Hongyue, interview, August 19, 2009)*

Teacher Hongyue was approaching collaboration in a "humble" and least intimidating way so as to sustain long-term relationships. That approach would have to be balanced with the demands of localization that the teachers under-took as described in the next chapter. The success of localization, according to activity theory, would require careful orchestration and collaboration between members of the teachers' communities including their colleagues and admin-istrators. However, as will be seen, the teachers were working mostly in their own "sandboxes" although the challenges they faced to undertake localization were quite similar across the board. Had they collaborated with one another and with other teachers, it is reasonable to speculate that the potential to overcome the challenges could have been greatly enhanced. Collaborations of all types and at all levels are essential as they allow "movement; they release tension; they create new mountains; they shake existing structures" (Wenger, 1998, p. 254). Like the activity of volcanoes, the process of collaboration generates both light and heat for the collaborators, but in the end it brings about fertile grounds for new growth.

# 7

# TAKING OWNERSHIP

## The Bridging of the Local with the Global in English Language Teaching

*Water far away will not put out fires close by.*

Our purpose in this chapter is to further understanding of how Western-trained Chinese English language teachers take ownership of their instruction by localizing information they have obtained from abroad while sustaining the use of what is most relevant in their own setting. In this way, we hope to contribute to an East-to-West flow of language teaching knowledge and practices to balance prevailing Western-centric perspectives on second and foreign language teaching.

As language educators, we have engaged in professional development activities with teachers across several institutions in the United States and in China and at different stages in their preservice and in-service teaching journeys. For the research reported here, we worked with experienced English language teachers Meiling, Fangxue, Lichang, and Hongyue 2 to 6 years after they had returned from the United States. Consequently, over a period of years they had been able to reflect on their education overseas and its impact on their English language teaching in China. They were among the fortunate 20% or so of Chinese English language teaching professionals who had been able to go abroad and develop a dual view of their own culture in conjunction with the foreign culture, which, along with their teaching expertise, made their experiences noteworthy.

We were particularly interested in these teachers' work in relation to the communicative language teaching (CLT) approach because it is the mandated approach in English language teaching in China (see chapter 4). As the discussion in this chapter will show, we found that they were not simply applying CLT but actively appropriating it, taking ownership of, and localizing it. They courageously assumed agency in creative ways by making decisions about what was workable in their classrooms and creating an effective blend of methods.

## Activity Theory Revisited

Before we describe the teachers' undertakings, it is warranted to revisit the theory that frames the description. In chapter 2, we explained why we have taken a sociocultural perspective in our research. Activity theory, which emerged from this perspective, helped to illuminate the Chinese English language teachers' progression through a series of experiences and contexts that influenced their understanding of the communicative language teaching (CLT) approach and how they could use it. That is, activity theory provided us with a lens (see Figure 7.1) through which to understand the process of "appropriation" and see how teachers (subjects) took ownership of and localized the CLT approach (object) and how this process was mediated by available resources in the context of local rules, community expectations, and existing structures (mediating tools). It also revealed how the conflicts and tensions inherent in the appropriation process led to the localization (outcome) of the CLT approach and its principles by the Chinese teachers we interviewed in ways that accommodated the uniqueness of their setting and the complexities of their students' needs.

As a key concept in activity theory, "appropriation" is defined as "a process through which a person adopts the pedagogical tools available for use in particular social settings … and through this process internalizes ways of thinking endemic to specific cultural practices" (Grossman, Smagorinksy, & Valencia, 1999, p. 15). We interpreted this to be the Chinese English language teachers taking ownership of the CLT approach and its principles by incorporating and juxtaposing them with the norms and practices of their schools and the larger Chinese social setting.

## The Ownership and Localization of the Communicative Language Teaching (CLT) Approach

In the following discussion, we use the paths outlined by activity theory to describe the processes by which Teachers Fangxue, Meiling, Hongyue, and Lichang appropriated and localized CLT in their classrooms.

### *The Subjects and Object: Chinese ELTs and Their backgrounds' Influence on the Appropriation of CLT Principles*

As subjects, the English language teachers made decisions as to whether and how to adopt and use the object, CLT, by drawing on their experiences in China, both before and after their educational sojourns in the West.

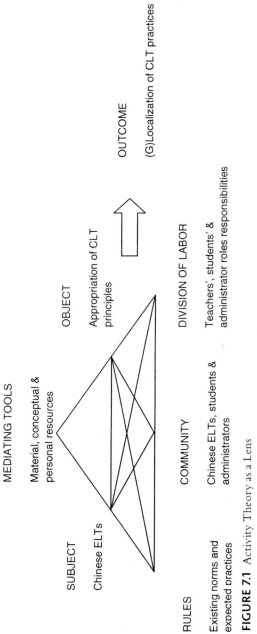

MEDIATING TOOLS

Material, conceptual & personal resources

SUBJECT

Chinese ELTs

OBJECT

Appropriation of CLT principles

OUTCOME

(G)Localization of CLT practices

RULES

Existing norms and expected practices

COMMUNITY

Chinese ELTs, students & administrators

DIVISION OF LABOR

Teachers', students' & administrator roles responsibilities

**FIGURE 7.1** Activity Theory as a Lens

*Teacher Fangxue and Student-Centered Learning.* Student-centered learning in CLT became an "umbrella" concept (*fàn chēng*) for Teacher Fangxue. Before going abroad to pursue his master's and doctoral degrees, Teacher Fangxue already had 10 years of teaching experience at both the secondary and university levels. During those years, like most Chinese teachers, he believed that he must take on the responsibility of "imposing" knowledge on the students in his classrooms. Teacher Fangxue considered the undertaking of this responsibility as not only essential but also as a noble duty. He recalled how he taught before going abroad:

> In the past, I just lectured, lectured, and lectured in class, and my students listened to my big speech. In an exhibitionistic style, I put all my efforts into showing them all that I knew. Basically, I was lecturing while they listened to me. It was my noble duty to lecture and their duty to listen.
>
> *(Teacher Fangxue, interview, May 22, 2009)*

However, his notion of teacher-centered instruction was challenged by his Western experience:

> After returning from the West, one radical change I had made was in my view of a teacher's role in the classroom. Before going abroad, I thought you were a qualified teacher if you had abundant knowledge. This was my deeply rooted idea. If you do not have abundant knowledge, you have no right to stand on the teaching platform. However, after experiencing Western education, I realized that the teacher is not the only source of knowledge in the classroom.
>
> *(Teacher Fangxue, interview, May 22, 2009)*

This realization made Teacher Fangxue more open to the CLT principle of student-centeredness (see CLT principles, chapter 4). He still saw complications in the principle, but as we will later see in this chapter, he could accept provisionally that making room for students' engagement and contributions in the classroom moved learning to a new place, where student investment and motivation were enhanced.

*Teacher Lichang and Scaffolding Learning.* For Teacher Lichang, supporting students' learning became a center point in her language instruction. However, she had begun her teaching career in China at a quite different point, by honoring her own mentors, trusting their wisdom, and modeling her teaching on their methods:

> Reading one sentence and explaining it—my previous teachers taught in this way and I taught like them too in the past because I had learned from

them. Every sentence had to be explained and analyzed very carefully, including its structural elements and key grammar points.

*(Teacher Lichang, interview, May 24, 2009)*

She was teaching primarily by repeating grammar knowledge, "always afraid," she added, "that students would not understand it." However, she came away from a 2-year TESOL program in New Zealand, where CLT was the dominant approach, with the perspective that instead of worrying whether students will "get it all," teachers should prioritize supporting and providing students with a sense of accomplishment and motivation to pursue objectives on their own:

> My whole belief on how teachers teach and how students learn changed. My biggest change was that my teaching should mean giving students an effective and easy way to understand so that they could achieve goals on their own. Really, making the subject matter accessible and doable, these ideas influenced me most.

Teacher Lichang experienced how her New Zealand teachers provided various forms of support whenever they invited their students to engage in a task, be it challenging or otherwise. Teacher Lichang consequently gravitated to the idea of scaffolding (see CLT principles, chapter 4) which she saw as central to instruction. For example, in her English writing class, she stressed the significance of a combination of direct instruction and modeling as a way to provide students with sufficient scaffolding:

> For example, I both told and showed them how I select topics, and then the students did it themselves. After the selection process, I told and showed them how I do research, including the literature review, and then they were able to follow the steps.
>
> *(Teacher Lichang, interview, May 24, 2009)*

She contrasted her approach with that of her colleagues who, according to her, "ask students only for products" but do not give enough guidance or time to complete what the teachers asked for.

*Teacher Meiling and Critical Thinking.*    For Teacher Meiling CLT's principles of critical thinking in communication were central, not just because of her Western education but also due to her early experiences growing up in an educated family that placed immense value on knowledge and its preservation. Her Chinese schooling experiences reemphasized these values, to which her experiences in an American master's program added a new dimension, an enhanced appreciation of extensive discussion opportunities and reflective papers to cultivate critical thinking. She was intrigued by how these assignments relied less on acquiring established knowledge and more on students taking ownership of learning and pushing it to a new place. In experiencing this emphasis herself, Teacher Meiling found that the assignments and the peer engagements in the American classroom had not left her much room to be the "silent" and "neutral" Asian student. The American learning environment forced her to assume positions on ideas and most of all to try to articulate the positions and demonstrate how they were meaningful to her, which led to her appropriation of this kind of critical thinking in her classroom:

> My biggest change is that the very important thing I currently do in my class is to ask questions, and they are problem-based questions, because I found that students are not able to think of questions…. They are always ready to listen to the teachers and always ready to take notes. So I just told them directly, "I do not need you to take any notes. I can make a copy of my notes for you…." I told students that books and theories are over there on the shelves, but the key issue is that they should be able to think critically right here with me. This is very important so they know why they are learning, don't you think so?
>
> *(Teacher Meiling, interview, May 21, 2009)*

Teacher Meiling's statement suggests that critical thinking assumed major importance in her instruction as a means to inject meaning and purpose as well as engagement into students' learning. She saw this emphasis as a main change brought about by her Western training.

*Teacher Hongyue and Purposeful/Meaningful Learning.*   Teacher Hongyue, in order to maintain purposefulness in students' learning, focused on teaching language through content. This way, she felt that her students would see the dual purpose of English-language learning as (see CLT principles, chapter 4) authentically contributing to both their language and their academic achievement simultaneously. Teacher Hongyue came to this position after spending an extended period of 6 years in Australia, which she saw as a major influence on changes in her instruction:

> Before I left for overseas, I thought that for the graduate students I was teaching, language was only a tool for communication, only a medium. Now I emphasize language for learning content. My 6-year experience in the West has influenced this change.
>
> *(Teacher Hongyue, interview, July 19, 2009)*

As an indication of the importance to her of appropriating content-based language instruction, after returning from the West, Teacher Hongyue developed a new course, Cross-Cultural Communication (a pseudonym) for graduate students who were mainly in-service Chinese English language teachers. In this course, she not only introduced authentic topics and issues in cross-cultural communication but also made the decision to teach the class entirely in English.

> For students at the graduate level, maybe their language foundations are different, some better, some worse, both were possible. However, since they have reached this level, they are interested to learn content, not just the English language, which they have already done in their undergraduate studies. Now they want content knowledge—they also want to advance to knowledge commensurate with their level; that is what keeps them interested, otherwise why would they come to an English class they already had in the past? According to my personal observations, the students kept good pace with me in English. If sometimes they could not do that, I repeated or slowed down.
>
> *(Teacher Hongyue, interview, July 19, 2009)*

Meaningfulness and purpose in language learning require a context of authentic and useful information. For the 40 graduate students in Teacher Hongyue's class, their maturity and extensive experiences made language learning for its own sake, without being useful to further their academic and professional knowledge, insufficient. In other words, they wanted not only *to learn language but also to use language to learn.*

The decisions of all four teachers to adopt and use specific CLT principles were informed by their backgrounds, their experiences in the West, and their changed perspectives upon returning to their Chinese classrooms. They were responsive teachers (Prabhu, 1990) who used all pedagogical tools available to them to foster student investment in learning.

### Mediating Tools

In activity theory, instead of dichotomization, there is a "seamless and dialectic relationship" (Lantolf, 2000, p. 79) between the mental and the social. Lantolf goes on to say that human relationships and artifacts mediate and regulate what goes on in our minds and what we do behaviorally as a consequence. In this section, we will focus on the material and interpersonal resources that mediated and thus affected the four English language teachers' thinking related to their adoption of CLT principles. In particular, the teachers' instruction was mediated by their use of authentic materials, questioning approaches, scaffolding frameworks and language, and interpersonal resources. We will then demonstrate how the teachers' undertakings led to the g/localization of CLT's principles in ways responsive to their settings.

*Authentic Materials.* These materials consisted of realia and materials readily available in the media, academic materials, and real-life examples. Instead of resorting to a single English textbook to be used by students majoring in multiple areas, Teacher Meiling chose documents containing current events and social, economic, and political topics such as newspapers, magazines, and government publications. When she started to teach in 2009, the Conference of the Chinese National People's Congress and the National Committee of the Chinese People's Political Consultative Conference were being held. She said that these two top legislature conferences, which were widely covered by the media, gave her a very good opportunity to select her class materials from various subjects and proposals being debated, all of which were controversial and strongly affected people's lives. Teacher Meiling selected them as powerful tools to promote students' critical thinking as concerned Chinese citizens while they discussed the issues in English:

> There were various topics that emerged during the two annual conferences. Many were social problems, and many of these still could not be solved according to the opinions from the experts participating in the conferences. I engaged the students in discussions of the topics, like the newly issued law on food safety, increased investment in education, and social welfare and health care.
>
> (Teacher Meiling, interview, June 23, 2009)

Teacher Meiling said it would have been easier to focus only on explaining language points in the materials, but she insisted that asking students to express their opinions, critique the experts' opinions and proposals, and offer their own solutions were more important for them as graduate students. These materials served as powerful mediating tools for her to promote not only critical thinking, but also, she hoped, social justice in the real world.

Similarly, Teacher Hongyue used authentic materials in her content-based English-language class, "Cross-Cultural Communication." In addition to readings from the research literature on the topic, she used her personal experiences as a student in Australia and her students' own experiences with cross-cultural communication as primary resources, as shown in her syllabus:

> In this course students will focus on improving their communication with people from diverse cultural backgrounds. The course is designed particularly for teachers, trainers, and others involved in promoting effective communication in situations of cultural diversity. We will use examples from our own experiences, and these examples will provide a context for what we will be reading on basic theories in intercultural communication, language and cultural values, and strategies appropriate in diverse contexts.
>
> (Teacher Hongyue's syllabus, July 2009)

The topics in Teacher Hongyue's class ranged from intercultural communication theories to nonverbal communication. She provided many examples of her own passage through the stages of euphoria, confusion, depression, adjustment, and acceptance as she transitioned into life in Australia over a period of 6 years. One of the examples she related involved her first experience of sitting on a bus next to two Australians and attempting to communicate with them. First, she asked whether they were "blacks," as in that early point in her life in Australia, she did not realize that the politically correct terms for the two individuals were either Indigenous Australians or Aboriginals. Second, when she asked them whether there were only two members in their family, she put two fingers out with her palm down, a polite way to gesture in China but evidently not polite in Australian culture, as she gathered from the reaction of the two people on the bus.

In response to her personal examples, Teacher Hongyue invited students to share cross-cultural communication examples from their experiences, both personal and professional. According to her, many of these teachers had frequently sought opportunities to speak English to improve their proficiency and thus had accumulated good fodder for discussions on intercultural communication.

Teachers Meiling and Hongyue used authentic texts and real-world examples to mediate their instruction thoughtfully and purposefully. This was similarly the case in the use of questions by Teacher Meiling and another teacher, as described in the following section.

*Questioning Approaches.*   Both Teacher Meiling and Teacher Fangxue used questions as mediating tools. Taking a problem-based questioning approach was essential in Teacher Meiling's efforts to engage students to think critically about real-life issues and problems in her English class, which began with provocative questions that generated substantive and critical thinking among her students. For example, one day she started class with the following questions: "What led to the situation described in today's story in the *China Daily* about this girl from a rural area whose chance to study at a university was snatched away by an imposter?" "What problems exist in Chinese educational systems that allow for such things to happen?" "What right do key and famous high schools have to ask for expensive admission fees?" "To what extent are public schools promoters of educational inequality by charging such fees?"

Teacher Fangxue also used questions, but primarily as a strategy to make his class student-centered. He based his lesson plans on various questions to prevent himself from falling into his previous approach of teacher-led drills and grammar explanations.

Teacher Fangxue's strategy was to expand the types and number of questions for each of the 10 units in a textbook titled *New Horizon College English* he was using with a class of 42 undergraduates, who were non-English major students. Each unit in the text provided six to eight "knowledge-based" or factual questions, as Teacher Fangxue described them, for which the answers were to be found in the text. He increased the questions for each unit to as many as 50, focusing on students' personal experiences and reflections. For example, in a unit on education, the knowledge-based questions in text included, "In these hard times, what are the major objectives of most students described in the text?" To this type of question, Teacher Fangxue added questions that directly penetrated students' own lives: "Why do you choose the subjects that you are taking?" "What does the phrase 'we can't have it both ways in life' mean to you?" "What is the meaning of education to you—Is it for your life or for your career or both?" Teacher Fangxue had students address these questions in pairs or in small groups, depending on what grouping students were comfortable with. These types of opinion-based questions were meant to open communications between students and most of all to take the focus away from Teacher Fangxue as the center of the class:

> Traditional text teaching was teacher-led translation, vocabulary, diffi-cult points, and language points. I am hoping for some improvement. For example, when I think of CLT, in teaching texts, students should lead the discussion, not just me. Opening it up to questions beyond what is in the text is always a part of all of this.... It is very important to create such an environment for students. This environment provided a lot of opportu-nities for students to speak and to lead discussions between themselves.
>
> *(Teacher Fangxue, interview, August 18, 2009)*

Another questioning approach Teacher Fangxue used to enhance student-centered learning was what he called "fishbowl conversations." Teacher Fangxue would designate three students as "experts" for the day. The three would sit in a circle, the fishbowl, while the other students sat outside. After Teacher Fangxue introduced a topic from the textbook, the "expert students" in the fishbowl discussed the topic for a few minutes. Then Teacher Fangxue would stop their discussion and invite other students to ask questions of the students in the circle. Student-centered activities such as the "fishbowl" conversations were aimed at bringing about students' active participation and authentic communication among peers while creating room for the teacher to retreat from the teaching platform as "a sage on the stage" and become a "guide on the side."

To support the student-centered elements, Teacher Fangxue gave them weight in his grading system, in which he allocated 30% to personal reflections and 25% to students' participation and attendance, comprising more than half the total course credit, and the rest to scores on standardized tests. By includ-ing multiple assessments in the overall grading for the course, Teacher Fangxue intended not only to provide a more comprehensive picture of students' perfor-mance and the outcomes in his student-centered classroom, but also to make the grades more meaningful to students.

*Language/Interpersonal Communication Resources.* Teachers Meiling and Fangxue also used verbal expression and interpersonal skills in appropriating the CLT principles of critical thinking and learning language through content.

For example, although English was the language medium of her course, Teacher Meiling explained that she did not express anger or disappointment when students asked her whether they could switch to Chinese in their conversations:

> If I forced students to only speak English, they would do a good job, but the feeling of wanting to express themselves would be hindered by the language. I did not impose that.... They spoke English spontaneously when it was easy. They took time to organize their English when what they were talking about was complicated. Either way, I did not force them to always stick to English; I thought both were ok, yes!

In appropriating the principle of student-centeredness, Teacher Fangxue was especially attentive to how he could foster a "harmonious" environment in his classroom. One way was to teach and practice the English of politeness; that is, the use of language to establish good relations among speakers. For example, he encouraged students to use polite exchanges such as "How are you doing today?" and "Good, good, and thank you" as a matter of daily classroom routine. Similar language smoothed communications in discussion, such as "Would you like to answer this question?" He also brought students' attention to expressions that reiterated the colearner role that everyone had in the class; for example, such expressions as "I learned a lot from your work today," "I did not realize that until you mentioned it," and "You added something new to my thinking."

Teachers Meiling and Fangxue were trying to achieve a particular mind-set and tone in their classrooms through such language and interpersonal communication resources as mentioned above. They understood the potential for the resources to have positive effects on classroom relationships and interactions, ultimately supporting the instructional goals they sought to achieve.

*Scaffolding Frameworks.*   As mentioned above, appropriating the scaffolding frameworks that supported students learning was important to Teacher Lichang. Specifically, Krashen's (1988) "i+1" concept of scaffolding learners to move from where they are (i) to the next level (1) impressed her greatly. She saw the concept as critical, especially as it provided step-by-step and recurring assistance. In her class of 40 sophomores majoring in multiple subjects, we saw her using several of the scaffolding approaches she encountered while studying in New Zealand.

One was the "4/3/2" (Maurice, 1983) approach to support students' speaking fluency through multiple practice sessions with different time limits and different student audiences. The approach entailed students giving a similar speech at three different and increasingly faster speeds (4 minutes, 3 minutes, and 2 minutes) to three different groups of classmates. By the third time, the aim was for students to be able to deliver their speech in a more succinct and less hesitant way than when they began.

Another conceptual model from the West that Teacher Lichang used was the process writing approach to support students' completion of short-term and semester-long writing projects. This approach involved students going through several stages of writing development with their peers. They would start with the prewriting stage in small groups, where students brainstormed, planned, and discussed their ideas. This was followed by students writing their first drafts and having their peers review and provide feedback on the drafts. The students then wrote second drafts based on peer feedback as well as self-edits. This second draft was reviewed one more time by peers before the students wrote the final draft. Teacher Lichang was encouraged by comments she received from several students who found the approach unique:

> The students said no teachers taught them this way before. I did it, step by step: students selected their own topics, discussed the literature, planned the research, and then wrote their first draft. They got feedback on the second draft and the final draft. The proof-reading was not done by me. I let students do it for each other, pair work and peer review.... I thought I used the process approach completely.
>
> *(Teacher Lichang, interview, May 24, 2009)*

In using these approaches, Teacher Lichang was scaffolding her students' English-language learning so that they could experience not only achievement but also autonomy in their own learning.

> All these procedures simplify the task. How can you teach without doing so? It would be "empty teaching." All these things make it easy not only for one student but for all students to learn and to do things by themselves.
>
> *(Teacher Lichang, interview, August 7, 2009)*

In essence, Krashen's concept and the scaffolding approaches that Teacher Lichang related to it provided her not only with conceptual ideas but also "pathways of practice" (Pawan & Groff Thomalla, 2005) that were aligned to what she felt was important in helping students develop as communicators, in speech and in writing.

These descriptions of how the teachers' appropriation of CLT principles was mediated by tools accessible to them demonstrate their agency in taking ownership of their instruction. However, their efforts were not unimpeded but were often challenged by conflicts, which led to further transformations of their instruction.

## Conflicts

According to Engeström (1987), an activity system is "a virtual disturbance-and-innovation-producing machine" (p. 11). Conflicts and contradictions are "historically accumulating structural tensions within and between activity systems" (Engeström, 2001, p. 137) and are a key part of activity theory. They have the capacity to create disturbances as well as push for innovations as outcomes.

We saw this dynamic at work in the experiences of these four Chinese teachers' appropriation of CLT principles. Conflicts resulted when the feasibility of the tools that they resorted to was impacted by the existing circumstances and infrastructure described at the bottom half of the activity theory triangle. Rules, policies, individual and communal belief systems, as well as the assumed nature of teachers' roles and responsibilities, were often sources of resistance that required accommodation.

*Rules, Policies, and Existing Infrastructure.* The conflicts in this category related to preexisting regulations and teaching conditions imposed upon the teachers. For example, Teacher Meiling faced the conflict of the nonalignment between her assessment approach and school rules and policies. She used multiple forms of assessment such as response papers, presentations, and final reflection papers to keep track of the students' progress and achievement while using authentic materials that she felt were aligned to generating discussions in CLT classrooms. She believed that her way of assessment was effective because "the students were learning through the whole process" (Interview, August 21, 2009). However, unlike Teacher Fangxue, who was able to incorporate multiple assessments in his grading system, Teacher Meiling ran up against the policies of the university where she taught, which required all the teachers to evaluate students using the formula of 1:2:7. This meant that 10% was for class attendance, 20% for the midterm examination, and 70% for the final examination. Teacher Meiling believed that this form of assessment could not test students' higher order and critical thinking skills, and she intended to use her own assessment, a situation that created great tension for both her and her students:

> The criteria for assessment I adopted and gave my students were not what the university required. I did not know when the university officials would discover it and how they were going to deal with me when they found out. I just let it go.... I cannot think about it as I will end up changing my assessment if they said I had to.
>
> *(Teacher Meiling, interview, August 21, 2009)*

Teacher Lichang ran into a conflict between her implementation of scaffold-and-process instruction and institutional examinations. There were two English exams every year: one was the regular final examination at the end of the semester, and the other was an annual national college English examination. The examinations did not allow room for her to incorporate any other forms of assessment, which would reflect the outcomes of her instruction. She described, for example, the conflict between her implementation of a portfolio assessment recording students' progress in process writing throughout the semester and her school's top-down control of the format of the final exam which has some semblance to Teacher Meiling's university scoring format as well:

> Throughout the semester, I promised my students that the portfolio was important, their final grade would be related to the whole learning process, and the final exam was only a means and would have just a very small percentage in my class. Unfortunately, our school required the unified standard: final test 60%, midterm exam 20%, and 20% for something else. So my whole promise did not work and had no effect.
>
> *(Teacher Lichang, interview, May 24, 2009)*

Several of our visits to Teacher Lichang's classroom also coincided with the school's administration of the National Band Four College English Test, which was a multiple-choice test of students' knowledge of grammar and reading as well as a structured test of their ability to write. By that time most of her colleagues had already stopped their regular English teaching and spent class time helping students practice for the test. Though Teacher Lichang continued her regular scaffolding and process writing teaching as usual, she felt the tension that resulted from knowing that her colleagues and students thought that she was wasting precious time by not preparing her students for the approaching English test.

There were also conflicts related to mandated time frames, classroom size, and content coverage. For example, rather than the anticipated complaints about limited access to authentic materials, Teachers Meiling and Hongyue raised the issue of limited time for using them fully. (We will be revisiting this conflict again in the following section on "student readiness.")

Teacher Hongyue brought up the conflict between her goals of engaging students in critical thinking and the mandated class size of about 40 students. The large number of students in a class made it challenging to undertake goals that required active engagement and give and take sessions between teachers and students. Also, the requirement that she cover all the topics listed in her syllabus led to more teacher-talk time than Teacher Hongyue wanted:

> I talked really too much. I dominated in talking too much. At that time I was only thinking to finish teaching all the content within the time limit.... There was so much content I needed to finish teaching.
>
> *(Teacher Hongyue, interview, August 19, 2009)*

Rather than reducing the quantity of the content of the course, she made the expedient decision to reduce her students' participation to save time.

Thus, the conflicts between the teachers' appropriation of CLT principles and the rules and policies of their institutions compelled the teachers to rethink their goals and their practices. Moreover, some of them also had to take their own deep-seated beliefs into consideration in relation to their CLT-based instruction.

*Beliefs about Teacher Classroom Authority and Comprehensive Knowledge.* Teachers Fangxue and Meiling had several conflicts in this area including those that pitted their Western influences against their instilled beliefs about teaching practice. Teacher Fangxue's classroom discourse revealed the conflict between his position on student-centered teaching and his belief in teachers as authority figures and main sources of knowledge in the classroom. For example, whenever he began or ended his explanations in class, he used sentences like "I will give you something," "I will provide you ...," "I will give you ways ...," and "This is what I wanted to give you today." These "I-give-you" statements indicate his predilection for teacher-to-student transmission of knowledge. The following dialogue between him and a student illustrates further his authoritative and teacher-centered stance in class:

| | |
|---|---|
| *Teacher Fangxue:* | What does a bachelor's degree mean for you? |
| *Student:* | I, I ... (Interrupted by the teacher) |
| *Teacher Fangxue:* | In 3 years, you will get your degree, right? |
| *Student:* | Yes. |
| *Teacher Fangxue:* | Bachelor's degree. What does it mean to you? |
| *Student:* | I... (Stopped by the teacher again while a few students laughed in a low voice) |
| *Teacher Fangxue:* | Does it mean you get what you want from the university? |
| *Students:* | No. (Laughing among students) |
| *Teacher Fangxue:* | No or yes? (Laugh), ok. So what do you want right now: knowledge, a moral sense, or the ability to solve problems in our society? What kind of things do you want? I gave you a choice: book knowledge, the ability to solve real problems, what do you want (lengthy explanation of the choices here)? So what do you want? |
| *Student:* | The second. |
| *Teacher Fangxue:* | I think a very good answer to this question should be what? I want both, right? I want both the knowledge and the ability, right? (Smiling) |
| *Student:* | (Nodding), yes. |
| *Teacher Fangxue:* | Sit down, please. |

*(Teacher Fangxue, class observation, June 3, 2009)*

The teacher's obvious dominance in this exchange was also evident during student presentations in his class. Rather than engaging students in a question-and-answer session about the presentations afterwards, Teacher Fangxue would immediately launch into his own presentations on similar topics for about one hour. We asked Teacher Fangxue why he did this:

The presentations were for the purpose of students practicing their abilities of expressing themselves, analyzing, and solving problems. However, I did not have 100% confidence in the student presentations. I needed to be sure we had the right information. Chinese students respect teacher's authority. They consider it right if it comes from the teacher's mouth, and they look down upon information if it comes from the students' mouths.

*(Teacher Fangxue, interview, June 5, 2002)*

Although Teacher Hongyue thought she should reduce some of her lecturing time in a content-based class that relied on the contributions of both the teacher and the students, she felt that the position conflicted with her belief that the teacher's authority and role as knowledge transmitter were critical in the Chinese context. In one of her interviews, she expressed her insistence on a strong teacher presence in her content-based language classroom due to her knowledge of the students as well as their own and society's expectations:

I knew these students, and I knew what they needed to learn. Here, in China, it is reasonable to require teachers to be knowledgeable.

*(Teacher Hongyue, interview, July 29, 2009)*

Remarks such as these reassert that Teachers Fangxue and Hongyue, despite their Western-based education, believed that for both them and their students a sense of confidence remained based on teachers' authority in the classroom and their grasp of information.

Given the situation, it is easy to understand Teacher Meiling's lack of confidence in her efforts to improve her students' critical thinking through the use of authentic materials. She felt that what stood in the way of this goal was her lack of content knowledge in students' fields of studies. Because of her students' wide range of academic backgrounds, such as administration, management, medicine, and public affairs, she felt she did not have enough content knowledge to push their thinking in those areas:

My current problem is that my background knowledge did not allow me to give students a glass of water because I did not have a bucket of water first.... I always had the tendency to focus more on education because that was my major. For other topics, I could not go in depth in my teaching because I did not know enough. I lacked the confidence.

*(Teacher Meiling, interview, June 2, 2009)*

In the cases of Teachers Fangxue, Hongyue, and Meiling, furthering their goals based on CLT student-centered principles would require that they reconsider their beliefs that teaching effectiveness depended primarily on teacher authority and comprehensive knowledge, a focus which contradicted the concept of student-centeredness as a way of supporting students' development of their own knowledge.

*Students' Readiness and Teachers' Roles and Responsibilities.*  Conflicts also emerged related to students' lack of readiness to meet teachers' expectations of them as active agents in their own learning, one of CLT's main principles.

The first conflict was related to students' readiness to undertake critical thinking. Teacher Meiling cited that one of the main causes of the conflict was the institutional time constraints that limited use of authentic materials, which required extensive reading as an important preparation for critical thinking. If students did not have enough time for reading the materials it was difficult for her to require them to articulate their positions. For the non-English-majors she taught, students might spend as little as 2 hours per week on English. Understandably, these circumstances hindered Teacher Meiling's efforts to push students to think critically in class:

> When I asked them questions, they could not answer because they did not read. I was thinking if they did have time to read and prepare for class [I could] design a different teaching method, on the basis of their preparation. In terms of the articles they read, I could have asked them to play the roles of citizens on one side, the government on the other side. They could then have chosen their stances to express their opinions. I would let them debate and discuss. The problem was that they could not do these activities at all because they did not have time to read.
>
> *(Teacher Meiling, stimulus-recall interview, August 21, 2009)*

Similarly, for Teacher Hongyue, although her students were in-service teachers of English, their lack of extensive reading was also due to the time constraints as the cross-cultural communication class was offered in an intensive session, 5 hours a day for 7 days, during the summer and winter vacations. Given the pressure of the compressed schedule, students did not have enough time or energy to read outside of class and so were not prepared to use the readings for reflecting on issues and sharing real-life examples.

> Yes, the majority of students did not read, did not read. We were always in a hurry, in a hurry to finish class.
>
> *(Teacher Hongyue, interview, August 19, 2009)*

Teacher Meiling also brought up the issue of students' readiness in terms of the conflict between her Western-based notions of critical thinking and her Chinese students' expectations of teacher-delivered knowledge. She assumed that critical thinking would involve classroom sessions of reflective thinking and active questions and answers in the classroom, in which students would regard it as their responsibility to articulate thoughts and opinions. However, for the most part students were silent or did not seem to comprehend the materials. More to the point, Teacher Meiling speculated that her students still considered language learning as their goal in an English-language classroom. She noticed that when students did engage in discussions, it was common for them to merely engage in "empty criticisms" (arguments without support and evidence), as a means to practice using the language. She felt her students did not see critical thinking ability as necessary for them to "survive" in their English class.

> In most cases, I asked questions and pushed them to think, to reflect, and to respond, but if I did not do that, they would not take the initiative.
>
> *(Teacher Meiling, interview, August 21, 2009)*

For Teacher Lichang, the conflicts emerged in students' lack of readiness to engage in peer-to-peer scaffolding and their reluctance to trust in the process writing approach. She believed, however, that peer-to-peer and collective scaffolding that students offered to each other when they worked together was important, and sometimes more important than what she could teach them directly. In her classes she made deliberate efforts to encourage her students to engage in mutual scaffolding:

> I let students look for the key structures and language points in the text, let them have a discussion, let them write. At any time, there were always two or more students working together, solving problems collectively.
>
> *(Teacher Lichang, interview, May 24, 2009)*

However, she found that her students were struggling with working on their own, as demonstrated, for example, by their inability to respond to questions when a particular exercise was over:

> Only a few individual students answered my questions on active sentences, and I found that I still needed to explain from the beginning again. From that, I realized I could not skip the procedure. The majority of students working together did not get the ideas behind the expressions and I had to explain it to them one more time.
>
> *(Teacher Lichang, interview, June 8, 2009)*

This conflict always made her feel hesitant in making decisions on how much peer-to-peer scaffolding should be a part of her class and how much she should engage in direct teaching.

While implementing the process writing approach instruction, Teacher Lichang realized that not all her students were ready to take it on because they neither liked this Western approach nor felt they needed it. When five students in her class told her that they did not want to partake in the process writing approach, she had to make adjustments although the results were undesirable:

> Some students had opinions, and they expressed their opinions to me— "Why do I have to write like this?" I had some discussions with them.

However, when students insisted on writing in the way they knew from before, and did not want to follow my way, I allowed them to do so. When I collected these students' work, there was a big difference: it was totally different when I compared their writings to the ones written by students who followed the process writing approach. From sentence structure, to essay structure, and logic, these students' writing problems were big.

*(Teacher Lichang, interview, May 24, 2009)*

Working out alternative ways to meet the needs of students who chose not to engage in the process writing approach took additional time but also provided the opportunity to show them the benefits of process writing:

I read their writings carefully, then helped them correct each error, and talked with them. After talking, I showed them the well-written essays of those students who followed my approach. I then asked them to make comments on those essays and to compare them with their own writing.

*(Teacher Lichang, interview, May 24, 2009)*

Nevertheless, running parallel lessons in Chinese classrooms with 40 or more students proved to be too time-consuming and unrealistic for Teacher Lichang to continue.

Similarly, Teacher Fangxue struggled with his students' lack of readiness to engage in student-centered activities such as leading discussions and initiating classroom exchanges:

When I ask the students questions, my expectation is the students will actively respond. However, often this is not easy to get from them. When I ask questions or discuss topics with them, they are not able to respond. I have to help them. When they do not have any reaction, I have to lead and lead them again.

*(Teacher Fangxue, interview, August 18, 2009)*

His students' unresponsiveness resulted in Teacher Fangxue reverting to teacher-centered instruction, which he had originally hoped to avoid, a move that left him conflicted between his conviction that his instruction should be student-centered and the realities of the classroom:

There is conflict between my lecturing and student-centeredness. Student-centeredness means that students should be given more opportunities to speak in class … but sometimes I talk too much … consciously and unconsciously, I have the tendency to go back to teacher-centered instruction. I realize that very clearly.

*(Teacher Fangxue, interview, August 18, 2009)*

Because of students' lack of readiness and unwillingness to engage in CLT approaches, the teachers' hoped-for appropriation of its principles did not always take off, requiring them to step back and reconsider their options. Their next steps would be to situate the appropriation of CLT principles in their actual contexts.

## Outcomes: Ownership and Localization

Activity theory allowed us to trace the progression of the four English language teachers through a series of experiences and contexts that influenced their understanding of CLT and how it could be adapted to the needs and expectations of their actual classrooms and students. In this section, we will discuss the localization of CLT principles in terms of the processes that Ramanathan (2006, pp. 132–137) proposed for re-visioning West-based TESOL approaches. The processes would involve interpreting CLT as (a) a decodable approach, containing multiple and fluid meanings; (b) relatable once content in its instruction is drawn from local sources; and (c) doable once its practices are amalgamated with existing local pedagogic practices. Though the localization moves described below validate ongoing practices by Chinese English language teachers and provide insight into the uniqueness of teaching the subject in China, they may also ring true in other contexts. It must also be noted that outside of the context of these Western-trained teachers, the localization of the principles may not always be recognized or accepted as aligning with Western-based conceptualizations of CLT. This is a discussion we will continue in the final chapter.

*Seeing CLT as Open-Ended.* Rather than seeing the approach as prescriptive and static, the Chinese English language teachers viewed it as amenable to reinterpretation and reconstruction in its principles and practice. There was an underlying realization that, similar to other approaches, CLT is "wrought by cultural codes and conventions" (Ramanathan, 2006, p. 132) in the place where it originated and is practiced.

> I think each culture has its own significance and influence. So in our teaching we should not just copy Western models as a whole. China has its own characteristics and ways of doing things although the West may have more freedom in what they want to teach and study.
>
> *(Teacher Fangxue, interview, May 22, 2009)*

By asserting their own cultural claims, the English language teachers expanded ownership of the Western-based approaches they valued at the same time they retrofitted these approaches to work in their own classrooms. We see instances of such ownership in the ways Teacher Meiling reconceptualized critical thinking in discussions and Teacher Fangxue altered his notion of student-centered instruction, two foundational CLT principles. For Teacher

Meiling, the reconceptualization was based on her students' limited experience with critical thinking and nonreadiness for a major move forward. She proceeded by exposing students to discursive texts in English and then weaving critical thinking into their comprehension activities as initial steps toward students developing their own critical voice:

> Students do not have many thoughts before they read. The majority of them need to know what others wrote and said. After reading other people's work, they begin to have their own ideas. I would have problems if I used Western critical thinking values.
>
> *(Teacher Meiling, interview, June 2, 2009)*

Nevertheless, Teacher Meiling explained that one of the challenges of taking this approach was the scarcity of suitable resources in English for students to read. The resources produced in China that she predominantly used did not always expose students to native speakers' critical perspectives or ways they expressed their opinions.

For Teacher Fangxue, the Western concept of student-centeredness challenged his beliefs in teacher authority, as was evident in his teacher-centered practices of lecturing and talking from the teaching platform. However, instead of worrying about violating the CLT principle that a teacher's main role is that of a facilitator rather than an authority, Teacher Fangxue decided that he would modify the student-centered principle to "guided student-centeredness." He explained the modification this way:

> I feel that here in China, teachers' function is bigger than that in the USA. The function of Western teachers is to guide students to think and to study, but not to be a source of knowledge. In China, teachers have dual roles: one you could see from where I stood at the front where I was the source of knowledge and the authority. But I am also the guide who asks questions and helps students to think actively.
>
> *(Teacher Fangxue, interview, June 5, 2009)*

Although Teacher Fangxue had to make modifications, he placed a high premium on teachers finding ways to encourage student-centeredness in their classroom. Although his modifications might have made his position in the classroom look very traditional to Western advocates of CLT, in fact he did not go entirely back to his previous teacher-centered instruction but found ways to introduce student-centered instruction into his repertoire in ways that were compatible with his setting and students.

Similarly, Teacher Hongyue held a high regard for student-centeredness, which she interpreted as being knowledgeable about what students needed and letting them know she cared about them:

> Though I was lecturing throughout the lesson, my words and gestures actually gave students some chances to participation which I know is important in CLT. They were a kind of an invitation. Sometimes it was my eye contact, or just questioning words at the end like "right?" "got it?" and "any questions?" Even when students only responded with a simple "yes" or "no," I did give them an opportunity to say something and I showed them I cared about their response.
>
> *(Teacher Hongyue, interview, August 19, 2009)*

Such reconceptualizations of the principles of critical thinking and student-centeredness may not converge with the CLT principles in the West, but to the Chinese teachers, they represented necessary first steps in the localization process. At the same time, the teachers remained appreciative of the changes that CLT and its principles were propelling.

Besides reconceptualizing principles, taking ownership to localize CLT also involved drawing from local content. In the discussion below, relevant sources and the reasons for their use are highlighted.

*Drawing Content from the Local.*   Personal relevancy and motivation were two reasons for using local resources in English language teaching. In her cross-cultural communication course, Teacher Hongyue was intent on immersing students in English learning through interesting and timely subject matter. As described earlier, she used examples from her experiences as an international student in Australia with the hope of eliciting personal examples from the in-service English teachers in her class.

> I felt I was very suited to teach this course. My experience can benefit students. There are many reference books available currently, but students cannot benefit much from those books. If I incorporate my experiences and feelings in the class, students will not feel that the content is too distant.
>
> *(Teacher Hongyue, interview, July 29, 2009)*

Teacher Hongyue's experiences abroad made her an excellent source of knowledge about intercultural communications, but her students could not always reciprocate as their intercultural experiences were limited. Almost 80% of China's English teachers have never traveled to English-speaking countries, and most of their experiences using English have been with other native Chinese speakers or internationals they come across in China with varying frequency. Teacher Hongyue herself shared that there were infrequent opportunities for her to communicate with English-language native speakers while in China so even her intercultural exchanges were limited. Consequently, she started by raising students' awareness of the conventions of communications that support their own cultural values in their classrooms, such as sustaining harmony in teamwork while encouraging competition. From this beginning, Teacher Hongyue moved into discussions of communication issues related to Chinese culture and traditions. This way, she felt, students were more grounded in what they knew best:

> We should consider the students' levels and needs in terms of content. For the topic of miscommunication between Chinese and Americans, I hope I can bring in more Chinese culture.
>
> *(Teacher Hongyue, interview, August 19, 2009)*

Teacher Meiling had already been drawing from authentic and local materials for her class. In response to her students' challenges in reading and engaging with the materials in class discussion, she prompted them to connect what they were reading with their personal experiences. For example, when one student shared an article he read on the failure of local authorities to take action, Teacher Meiling prodded him to relate the article to his own attempt to gain the support of the authorities. The article, titled "Should the Suicidal Jumper Be Punished?" was about a Chinese man who was about to jump from a bridge into a river due to the pressure of owing 4,500,000 yuan (about U.S.\$723,000) in his failed construction project. The man was about to commit suicide after local authorities refused to help him find ways to pay the debt. At that point, instead of attending to the man's desperate psychological state, policemen at the scene charged him with disturbing public order by assembling a crowd to witness his jump from the bridge.

Although the student did not speak very fluent English and his handout contained grammatical mistakes, he touched on the serious topics of local law enforcement officers' lack of training in handling situations of self-endangerment and of the lack of local government oversight and regulation of construction deals in the city. He then continued to relate this topic to his own experience as a student, albeit on a smaller scale, of asking the local authorities for help reducing noise from a construction site at his university. His effort failed because no one he contacted was willing to listen and take responsibility to help solve the problem. The student ended by saying that when it came to issues of commercial interests, local authorities turned a blind eye, and it was the common people who paid for the problems that resulted in the end.

Teachers Hongyue and Meiling did not teach English only for its own sake, but created some situations in which students could apply their thinking skills to their own realities beyond the English classroom. By encouraging students to talk about larger issues in light of their own situations, the teachers also highlighted the importance of developing critical personal perspectives. Most of all, the teachers were focused on engaging students to view learning English as meaningful rather than intimidating and as a tool for intellectual growth:

> My goal is to let them feel that English is not a scary thing, but something important for ideas. The key is that they have to be interested.
>
> *(Teacher Meiling, interview, June 23, 2009)*

By drawing on local content, the teachers were moving toward the integration of what they learned in the West with local knowledge and concerns. These moves toward synthesis are discussed in the next section.

*Amalgamating CLT with Existing Chinese Pedagogic Practices.* In our final discussion of localization, we turn to the juxtaposition of CLT and Chinese pedagogic practices. This discussion is different from chapter 6, where we touched upon reasons why such venerable Chinese pedagogic practices as memorization, recitation, group reading, and translation continue to be prominent in English-language classrooms. In this section, we will describe several examples of how these practices were employed in tandem with CLT's established practices.

We begin with the example of Teacher Lichang's approach of combining her scaffolding practices including process writing with teaching to the test. She did not see the two as incompatible but as meeting different needs. She believed her combined approach would provide students with real skills to face and pass the tests:

> My teaching was not just test-driven. When students asked me whether they needed to practice test writing samples so that they could reproduce something similar on actual tests, I reminded that them that, "You already have the ability to finish writing 50 words in 5 minutes in my class, and so you should able to finish writing 120 words in half an hour on the tests."
>
> *(Teacher Lichang, interview, May 24, 2009)*

Additionally, instead of having them memorize samples, she provided them with an essay macrostructure (introduction, details and supportive arguments, counterarguments, conclusion) for the students to fill in with their own ideas in preparation for the essay tests.

Teacher Lichang thus aligned her scaffolding instruction with assisting students' efforts to pass tests and in this way supported both their English learning and their chances for success on the examination:

> Before going abroad, I was a test-driven teacher, and I would spend the whole semester helping students prepare for the test. If you want to get tenured, your students have to pass the Band Four test. The test is also very important for the students obviously. Now I do not teach for the sake of test only but I do not mean that I do not care whether my students could pass Band Four or not. I just feel that if my students improved their

English proficiency through my new teaching methods, the Band Four Test should not be a problem for them.

*(Teacher Lichang, interview, August 7, 2009)*

Her goal echoes the message of the Chinese version of the familiar aphorism: "Giving someone a fish is not as helpful as teaching the person how to fish." Taking this approach also clarified Teacher Lichang's main teaching goal: to improve students' ability through developing their autonomy as learners.

Another example of instruction that combines CLT principles and Chinese teaching practices is Teacher Meiling's juxtaposition of critical thinking with memorization and recitation. Although the former requires students to go beyond exploring and synthesizing to taking positions and testing those positions, either vicariously or through taking action, Teacher Meiling felt that her students needed to focus on articulating the positions they identified in the readings as a first step toward developing their own critical voices:

Students do not need to cite references for their ideas. Students just have to internalize what they read and then externalize it.

*(Teacher Meiling, interview, June 2, 2009)*

However, as we saw above, following this stage Teacher Meiling pushed students to take their own positions by relating what they read to personal experiences and real life circumstances in their society. In this way, Teacher Meiling created two steps for her students to take toward achieving critical thinking in their English-language communications.

Similarly, Teacher Fangxue was looking for ways build a bridge between student centered instruction and Chinese practices, to create what he called "CLT with Chinese characteristics." This aim was evident in the way he combined lecturing with posing opinion-eliciting questions to facilitate and guide student participation. In his stimulus recall interview he also declared that, as the newly promoted vice-dean, he would encourage teachers under his supervision to pay attention to balancing teacher talk with student talk:

So in the future I am trying to work out some ways to deal with this shortcoming of too much teacher's talk by limiting and regulating it. For example, teachers can only lecture for 15 minutes in class and they should give students 30 minutes to discuss. However, teachers cannot let students talk randomly, but they have to guide students in ways similar to my question-answer activity.

*(Teacher Fangxue, stimulus interview, August 18, 2009)*

Acknowledging the conflict between his intentions and practice pushed Teacher Fangxue to examine his deepest beliefs and convert inconsistencies into complexities. As a result, he included more student-centered techniques in his teaching while maintaining his core conviction about the role of the teacher as sanctified in Chinese culture. By opening windows if not doors to student participation, he found a reasonable path to positive change, which in his administrative role he would now lead others to follow.

Like Teacher Fangxue, conflict also led Teacher Hongyue to think about ways to combine lecturing with eliciting student participation, primarily by showing that she not only was open to student input but valued it, although she also remained mindful of her responsibility to fully deliver the instruction promised in the syllabus.

> I think students should participate in no matter what type of class if the condition allows it, but the degree will be different.... I will let students talk more. I should leave a little more time. A little more pause after each question, just a little more but not too much, otherwise, I cannot finish the plan for the day.
>
> *(Teacher Hongyue, stimulus recall interview, August 19, 2009)*

We saw from observations that lecturing continued to dominate Teacher Hongyue's instruction. However, she explained that she had synthesized the dichotomy of teacher- vs. student-centered instruction into what she termed "learning-centered instruction." From this perspective, the issue was not who was talking the most but whether the students were learning something new and understood how it impacted their lives.

> We introduced many Western theories to students all the time, but we can teach them how to combine those with what we do in a practical Chinese context. A good teacher will do well in combining the two.
>
> *(Teacher Hongyue, interview, August 19, 2009)*

Teacher Hongyue's statement aptly sums up the premise of localization. If students were learning in a way that is meaningful to them, the classroom goals would have been achieved. This principle was the reference point for her instructional decisions, not only regarding allocation of class time but also supporting change and stability together.

## Conclusion

The four Chinese English language teachers in this study were exceptional in that they were among the 20% who experienced being educated both in China and in a Western English-speaking country, which gave them insight into the dynamics of classroom teaching in both settings. They were able to use their dual experience to make sense of what was relevant to them as teachers and, most saliently, to their students within the Chinese institutional and societal contexts. As our description of the teachers' efforts in appropriating, taking ownership, and localizing CLT shows, their Western education had a significant impact on them. Nevertheless, they took the helm in selecting and adapting what was most meaningful to them and making it relevant in their context.

The four themes in activity theory, appropriation, mediation, conflicts, and outcome, provided us with an effective analytic tool to explore the activities of the four Western-trained Chinese English language teachers and their local settings simultaneously. We should note here that the term *appropriation* in activity theory is used differently from Grossman et al.'s (1999) five levels of appropriation ("1. Lack of appropriation, 2. Appropriating a label, 3. Appropriating surface features, 4. Appropriating conceptual underpinnings, and 5. Mastery," pp. 16–18), in that the latter equates appropriation with various levels of successful adoption of the original construct whereas activity theory conceptualizes it as a dynamic, interactive process that results in change. Grossman's levels were not appropriate for this study because they imply a performance checklist that is "assimilative" and "applicative" in orientation and does not acknowledge teachers' contributions in appropriation.

As we have documented throughout this chapter, the Chinese English language teachers were active in making deliberate decisions in their processes of appropriating CLT principles. In doing so, they approached appropriation with agency to initiate actions that were responsive to elements in their sociocultural context and took responsibility for their consequent impact. We take particular issue with Grossman's mastery level, which implies that once teachers have conceptually understood a particular tool, they will adopt all of its features, thus protecting the integrity of the original rather than flexibly using it to suit particular circumstances. As we mentioned at the beginning of this chapter, the Chinese English language teachers took agency in interpreting CLT as well as in selecting and combining its principles with what was most relevant and most desired at home. As we saw it, this was the teachers' way of using "distant waters to put out local fires and at the same time quench local thirst."

# 8

# CHANGING FROM EARTH TO SKY

New Policies and the Ever Changing Roles
of Western-Trained Chinese English Language
Teachers

*Reaching the heavens with one stride.*

China is a country on the move. When one asks people about what is taking place in their nation today, two expressions are likely to be heard: *rì xīn yuè yìng* or "things are changing day by day," and *fān tiān fù dì* or "unprecedented changes have already begun." In other words, the course of the future has already been altered. This is certainly the case in teacher education. As we mentioned in chapter 5, rapid changes are being heralded by two governmental documents: the 12th Five-Year Plan for National Economic and Social Development (NESD) (2011–2015) (China Direct, 2011) and the Outline of the National Long-Term and Short-Term Education Reform and Development Plan (2010–2020) (Outline, 1020.). Of the two, the "Outline" (*gāng yào*), provides strategic planning and specific guidance.

In this chapter, we will discuss the changes being promoted by the Chinese government's plan and vision, particularly as they are stated within the Outline, and how they are in tandem with the new teacher roles we see emerging based on our research on Western-educated Chinese English language teachers.

## Overall National Reform Objectives

The 12th Five-Year National Plan (NESD), endorsed by the People's Republic of China's (PRC) National Congress in March of 2011, represents a seismic shift from previous plans. Its goal is to achieve China's transition from dependence on other countries through its exports to increasing consumption from within its populace of 1.3 billion (Roach, 2011). In this way, the plan is intended to lead China to economic independence with a backbone of seven industries that promote sustainable growth rather than "growth at any cost" (APCO, 2010, p. 2). These industries are identified as "biotechnology, new energy, high-end equipment manufacturing, energy conservation and environmental protection, clean-energy vehicles, new materials, and next-generation IT" (APCO, 2010, p. 3). Additionally, it is a plan for "inclusive growth" or "prosperity for all in a harmonious society" (*hé xié shè huì*). The plan is a 30-year leap from Deng Xiaoping's policy in the 1980s of promoting *xiān fù* (getting rich first), which applied mainly to people in the eastern coastal regions, to the policy of *gòng tong fù yù* (common prosperity), advocated by China's past President, Hu Jintao, and Premier Wen Jibao (Fan, 2006), as well as the current President, Xi Jinping, who aims to continue the work of his immediate predecessors (Bradsher, 2013). Finally, the NESD is an action plan to maintain a 7% growth rate over the next 5 years in all aspects of economic and social development across regions and ethnic and ability groups. The plan comes at a time when moderating the effects of the global financial crisis is not only strategic but a necessary goal as well.

NESD's proposed goals are monumental in scale, and at this early stage of implementation, success is still to be hoped for. There is a Chinese proverb, "If heaven created man, earth will find a use for him," and our take on this proverb is that if the Chinese government created these educational plans, then it is the duty of Chinese educators to find good use for them and carry them out.

This sequence of Chinese 5-year plans provides an overview of the historical context from which the latest plan emerged. It also shows how economic rationales have changed over time in response to current contingencies, creating the necessary flexibility for timely change. Following is a discussion of the role of education in the current plan.

**TABLE 8.1** China's Five-Year Plans

| Plans | Dates | Key Features |
|---|---|---|
| First | 1953–57 | Stalinist Central Plan |
| Second | 1958–62 | Great Leap Forward |
| Third | 1966–70 | Agricultural Push |
| Fourth | 1971–75 | Cultural Revolution |
| Fifth | 1976–80 | Post Mao (Reforms and Opening Up) |
| Sixth | 1981–85 | Readjustment and Recovery |
| Seventh | 1986–90 | Socialism with Chinese Characteristics |
| Eighth | 1991–95 | Technical Development |
| Ninth | 1996–00 | State-owned enterprises (SOE) Reforms |
| Tenth | 2001–05 | Strategic Restructuring |
| Eleventh | 2006–10 | Rebalancing Alert |
| Twelfth | 2011–15 | Pro-Consumption |

*Source:* MSIM cited in Roach, 2011.

## Educational Reforms in Human Resource Development through Education

Human resource development through education is central in the Outline as China aims to develop what it calls a "learning society," composed of a prosperous, well-educated, and skilled citizenry. This goal is in line with the new emphasis on local spending and appreciation for homegrown goods. However, people's appreciation for those goods depends not only on increased affordability but also on increased confidence that the goods are produced by qualified workers in a system that reliably ensures their quality. Thus the development of human resources through education is essential for China, through the NESD, to move away from its long-standing image as the "world's factory" (APCO, 2010, p. 2) providing the cheap labor of workers with limited education, to that of being a world center with an educated and technologically advanced labor force by the year 2020. The Outline's other priorities, which include education being guaranteed in the national budget as the key in reform and innovation, essential to social stability and equality, and necessary for quality maintenance, all support the essential role of human resource development.

To reach its goals, the country is said to be spending $250 billion a year on educating its "human capital" (Bradsher, 2013). One of the Chinese government's objectives is to increase educational expenditure from 3.17% of the national budget in the 1960s to 4%, a level that has now reached 3.32%. This increasing investment puts teachers on the front line. The government points to its success in increasing the number of teachers from over a million in 1949 to almost 17 million in 2008. With the next cycle of information, they hope to report a further increase in educational expenditure and teacher numbers, which is necessary to achieve the government goal of 90% high school completion and 20% tertiary education completion by 2020, which would result in 195 million community college and university graduates (Bradsher, 2013).

Within the overall focus on human resources through education and the budgetary goals to achieve it, the Outline specifies strategic aims and reflects the overall direction of the Chinese educational reform.

## Strategic Aims in Education

The reform movement calls on educators to look both inwards and outwards. There are five strategic aims, three of which focus on expanding and popularizing education within China and the remaining two on improving and modernizing it by looking outwards. These correspond to trends in the types of teacher roles and responsibilities we found emerging in our research.

With regard to aims focusing on internal reforms, there is a push for increasing the number of preschool to high school years from 12.4 to 13.5 years. Concomitantly, the quality of the labor force is expected to improve by a rise in the level of education among workers from an average of 9.5 to an average of 11.2 years, This focus on workers via more widely distributed educational opportunities indicates that China is moving away from its past emphasis on the education of the elite to emphasizing mass education (Mohrman, 2008). Some urgency is expressed in developing "citizen friendly" education in which there is equitable educational access for the poor as well as the rich, for rural as well as city dwellers, for migrants as well as residents, and for the differently as well as the fully abled. Finally, education is also to be regarded as a lifelong enterprise with the government aiming for a 50% participation rate in continuing education and professional development while employees are in service.

These internal aims are accompanied by two equally significant aims, the fourth being a focus on reforming and modernizing education by looking beyond Chinese shores to build a modern, world class educational system that meets the highest global standards. This enterprise, however, is to be grounded in a firmly held Chinese perspective, a position captured in the expression, reform with "Chinese characteristics" (jiàn quán chōng mǎn huó lì de jiào yù jī zhì; which is commonly used to indicate that all innovations will be shaped to the present Chinese sociocultural, economic, and political context. In other words, reforms are to align with developments in the outside world while keeping in mind that the central government has a firm grip on the reins. Despite this caution, the fifth aim goes one step further to elevate educational standards and international competitiveness to a new level, for which innovation and creativity are to be encouraged. Hence, despite the constant caveat to maintain Chinese characteristics throughout the process of reform, it is clearly evident that the emphasis in these two reform aims is for education to be outward-looking and global in perspective so that the nation will be on equal footing with and eventually lead the world in productivity and expertise.

How do these aims in the Outline align with emerging teacher roles and responsibilities? This question is the focus of the next section.

## Alignment of Western-Educated Chinese English Language Teachers' Roles and Responsibilities with New Policies

As we examined the roles and responsibilities that emerged from the impact of Western language education programs on the Chinese English language teachers we interviewed, the ways in which they coincided with the policy priorities in the Outline became evident. As we saw in chapter 6, their Western-based education enabled the teachers to develop a dual understanding of both the Western and Chinese philosophies and approaches, including both their strengths and their weaknesses. This comprehensive view empowered the teachers to take a critical perspective on what was valuable to draw from each place and in particular to validate what the teachers knew should be preserved in terms of Chinese ways of knowing and practicing. Besides exposing them to new ideas, being abroad provided the distance from which to analyze the value of their own intellectual heritage. This experience enabled the teachers to be responsive "reclaimers of the local" (Canagarajah, 2005) who could confidently assess local knowledge and practices as valid given the circumstances of their settings, and more importantly, be supportive of their students' English learning. Privileging local knowledge as the context for incorporating imported knowledge, the teachers understood, would expand the scope while maintaining the relevancy of education. In this way, teachers could pursue the strategic aims of helping people to continue to see education as beneficial and accessible, to strive to gain entry into it, to stay longer in school, and finally, to continue to develop their expertise throughout their careers,

As discussed in chapter 6, the teachers faced many challenges in their efforts to reconcile the disjuncture between what they had learned in their Western programs and what was in place at home, and to change the status quo by building bridges between CLT and existing Chinese pedagogy. As "bridgers," they sought to bring together what they thought was the best of both worlds, but this amalgamation of the new and the traditional was often not welcomed by colleagues. Nevertheless, while remaining grounded in Chinese English-language pedagogies, they persisted in finding ways to bring them more in line with the principles of CLT, which prevail in much of the second and foreign language teaching world. In this way, the teachers undertook responsibility for modernizing education in keeping with the strategic aims articulated in the Outline.

Most importantly, these Chinese ELTs reported that their Western education had given them the confidence to take ownership of their own teaching. This was the core of our discussions of their localization of CLT's principles reported in chapter 7. Their localization reiterated Prabhu's (1990) conceptualization of a teacher's "sense of plausibility." Their localization practices did not entail seeking perfect methods but rather undertaking the challenge of creating a sense of involvement and investment in learning in their classrooms. This notion of teacher plausibility prioritizes teachers' insider knowledge of themselves as learners, of the sociocultural context in which they work, and of learners and their learning processes. In that sense, the teachers were "users and creators of knowledge and theorizers in their own right" (Johnson, 2006, p. 241). The teachers' assumption of these roles resonated with the goals of the Outline that stress innovation and creativity among teachers to lead the new generation of learners and leaders. By assuming CLT ownership through localization, the teachers demonstrated that, despite challenges, they were already taking up the call with agency and confidence.

## Teacher Education for Teachers of the "90 *hòu*" Generation: The Case of Yunnan Normal University

The "90 *hòu*" generation (people born during the 1990s), can expect to see changes in the way teachers are trained as per the goals of the 12th Five-Year Plan and the Outline strategic aims. We describe here the efforts of one teacher education university, Yunnan Normal University (YNU). The university is situated close to the source of the Mekong River in a Chinese province that shares 2,500 miles of international borders with Burma, Laos, and Vietnam. The University aims to be a "bridge tower" (*qiáo tóu bǎo*) connecting China to those countries (YNU, 2011, p. 11), in particular through education. This is evident in several of its eight main initiatives, which we obtained from a 2011 YNU report on its 12th 5-year plan efforts. Overall, the initiatives are aimed at "using talents to strengthen the power of school" (*rén cái qiáng xiào*) (YNU, 2011, p. 11). As the largest group of students trained in the university, teachers are the target of these initiatives.

The first strategic initiative is a project to encourage young teachers within Yunnan Province to pursue higher education abroad. This is followed by an emphasis on YNU collaborating with foreign universities to improve young teachers' teaching and research abilities. In that regard, they offer opportunities for scholarships and financial assistance for teachers to pursue pre- and in-service training and to seek mentorships to become visiting scholars in foreign countries. Young teachers are also encouraged to pursue academic degrees, such as doctorates abroad (YNU, 2011, p. 11).

Given its proximity to the Mekong subregional, South Asian, and Southeast Asian countries, YNU's second initiative is to support the development of a two-way talent base comprised of young Chinese teachers who can serve in those countries and also young teachers from those countries who can serve in China. One of the conduits for this initiative is the English language teacher training program, which in the past has required preservice teachers to acquire a European language such as German or French in addition to English. That requirement has now been changed to requiring that instead teachers learn a language from one of the neighboring countries. Along the same lines, to be inclusive of its neighbors as well as to expand the scope of the internationalization of its offerings, YNU changed the name of its English Teaching Methodology course to Foreign Language Teaching Methodology.

If implemented, these changes and many more will result in the development of cadres of talented international and interdisciplinary research and teaching teams of teachers. The teams will benefit from a diversity of pedagogical expertise and teaching know-how.

## Pulling It All Together

Discussions in this book have demonstrated that the teachers we worked with experienced an immense impact from their Western education. Using socio-cultural theory as a lens, we were able to understand this impact as it pertained to teachers' knowledge of themselves as learners in the West, knowledge of their students, and finally, knowledge of the school and social context in which they worked. Activity theory, on other hand, provided us with the means to trace the process by which the teachers relied on this knowledge to take owner-ship of the principles of CLT by localizing their implementation with Chinese characteristics. Finally, these findings and our analysis of the Chinese govern-ment's educational goals provided an indication that the teachers' Western edu-cation well-positioned them to be front-line reformers in meeting these goals.

A complex picture of the impact of Western education has therefore emerged from this book. The Chinese English language teachers did not think the West got it right all the time. They did not perceive Western theories and pedagogies as prescriptive knowledge they had to apply in their own teaching contexts. Rather they viewed their training interpretively, as a lens through which they could reevaluate and rethink their own knowledge, their profession, and who they were as English language teachers. Also, contrary to previous studies that emphasized the disjunctures between teachers' overseas education and their work at home, our research demonstrated that the teachers had agency in their learning as professionals and were consistently evaluating their training in light of their classroom realities in China. None of them fell into the dichotomy of either accepting or rejecting their Western teacher education; instead, they were very aware that empowerment and challenges coexisted all the time in what they were attempting to do, and that it was their responsibility to come up with language pedagogy that combined "global appropriacy and local appro-priation" (Kramsch & Sullivan, 1996, p. 199). In this regard, the findings in this research complicate the East/West binary argument that often emerges in CLT research that claims CLT is either practiced or not practiced by ELTs outside the West (Karavas-Doukas, 1996; Sato & Kleinsasser, 1999). The find-ings also challenge the argument of clear-cut contradictions between Western-based CLT and Chinese traditional teaching methods. Instead, we saw how the teachers acknowledged the relevance of aspects of both in their settings.

Nevertheless, the teachers' voices included in this book echo much that has been reported in the literature on the discrepancy between Western training and Eastern classrooms. The challenges the four Western-trained Chinese teachers faced after returning from abroad were consistent with research on contextual constraints on CLT implementation in non-Western settings (Burnaby & Sun, 1989; Chowdhury & Ha, 2008; G. Hu, 2002; Hui, 1997). Two points stand out: one, as discussed throughout this book, is that simply transplanting an approach developed in one setting into another is an uninformed practice almost sure to fail. The other is that deeply embedded constraints in Chinese English-language learning contexts continue to stand in the way of communicative language instruction and learning. They include students' focus on knowledge accumulation rather than problem-solving, their limited exposure to English, their lack of access to speakers of English, and their unclear purposes in learning English. With regard to teachers, constraints include their lack of training in and understanding of CLT, their unrelenting adherence to familiar beliefs and practices, and locally trained English language teachers' resistance to collaboration with Western-trained colleagues. In terms of the larger infrastructure, stumbling blocks include the Chinese government's high-handed involvement with school and instructional affairs, frequent policy changes, and preference for test-oriented curricula, all of which discourage instructional innovation.

Our work with the Chinese English language teachers and discussions of how to interpret the rich and complex data we collected also raise many questions. One central question is the extent to which CLT or other theoretical frameworks can be altered before their language learning and teaching goals are effectively undermined. This question is especially relevant to the contextual constraints that the four Western-trained Chinese English language teachers experienced upon their return home. Could these constraints be so limiting as to erode the theoretical legitimacy of the ways teachers practiced the approaches brought from abroad? Did the constraints frustrate the teachers to the point that they gave in to the status quo? These issues of theoretical integrity and situational constraints are at the heart of any cross-cultural translation of teaching methodologies, and researchers have only begun to understand the complexities involved and the challenges to be confronted.

## Professional Development: Reflections and a Suggested Model for Chinese English Language Teachers

How do discussions in the book impact the professional development of language teachers? For one, these persistent constraints need to be a part of discussions in Western-based teacher education programs that aim to have international relevance. Instead of ignoring the dramatic global variation of classroom contexts, these programs need to infuse teacher insider knowledge from multiple perspectives into traditional teacher professional development programs, which have been criticized for having a disproportionate focus on Western-based issues and perspectives (Johnson, 2006). The inclusion of teachers' insider knowledge as a formal part of teacher training requires the field's acceptance of "inquiry into teachers' experiences as mechanisms for change in classroom practices" (Johnson, 2006, p. 241) and teachers' ways of knowing as a legitimate form of scholarship. It is only then that teachers will find their training to be in accord with their experiences and central to their theorization of what it means to teach effectively.

In light of our work, we feel that any reform in teacher education should include an emphasis on teacher reflections. Reflective teaching has become the focus of efforts to bridge the gap between teaching theory and practice. Recognition of reflective teaching is the recognition of the value of teacher insider knowledge (Bailey, Curtis, & Nunan, 1998; Korthagen, 2001) to building linkages between what teachers know and their "pathways of practice" (Pawan & Groff Thomalla, 2005, p. 685). The teachers whose voices are present in this book were invited to reflect on what they did and on what worked or did not work for them. During the reflections, we saw their understanding of their pedagogy progress as they unpacked the meaning of their own experiences. This reflective process made them aware of things they might never have noticed without the chance to look over their teaching. In a word, engaging in reflections allowed the teachers to make their knowledge visible to themselves and to others (Richards, 2009).

The analysis and interpretation involved in writing this book also reaffirmed to us the value of teacher reflections in professional development. In related research, the second author, Faridah Pawan, along with Wenfang Fan of Tsinghua University, identified the benefits of teacher reflection practiced in mandated collaborative groups *(jiàoyánzǔ)* or individually (Pawan & Fan, 2013). Although we did not find precise divisions among Van Mannen's (1977) three levels of technical, practical, and critical reflections, our data demonstrated the potential of these two types of reflective settings to yield different types of knowledge. Collaborative group reflections were mainly concerned with technical matters pertaining to classroom instruction, while individual reflections focused primarily on social-historical-political-cultural knowledge. Even at this early point in this research, it was evident that peer- and self-reflections served different but useful complementary roles in English language teachers' learning and professional development.

The importance of teacher reflections in professional development led the first author, Pu Hong, to include them in her modifications of activity theory, which led to the development of her pedagogical localization process model described below.

This model changes the perception that teachers' pedagogy localization is the outcome of a linear process to the recognition that localization is recursive and circular. As teachers reflect, construct knowledge, and further reflect, the four components of this model, appropriation, mediation, tensions, and localization, interact continuously. Pu Hong stresses that the key to this model is uncovering this dynamic process of knowledge development, which, in this discussion, characterizes how four Chinese English language teachers localized what they learned in Western institutions.

As we end this chapter, we are reminded again of wise Chinese maxims, and particularly two that seem to address our situation. The first offers words of caution applicable to this chapter on policies: "heaven's laws are so easy to

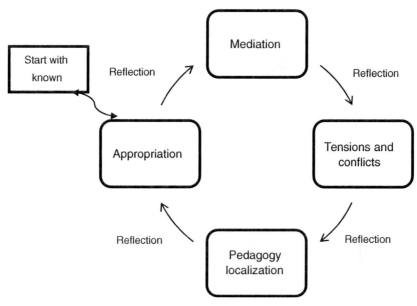

**FIGURE 8.1**  Pu's Pedagogy Localization Process Model

accept but so hard to abide by." In terms of our teachers' efforts overall, we give them our continued faith and encouragement that their hard work will achieve, not the impossible, but rather realistic benefits of what is sent from the "heavens," because, as the second maxim says, "a heavenly miracle is not achieved when one can walk in air or on water but when one can walk on earth."

# 9

# A VIEW FROM THE MOUNTAIN

## Teachers' Personal Reflections

*Jade is only stone until it is polished.*

The proverb above suggests that for people to reach their fullest potential, education is essential. In this chapter, we also take the proverb further to mean that the significance of what the four Chinese English language teachers learned in the West would only be evident if its impact is subject to analysis. In this sense, the Western education that the English language teachers received was made meaningful by the way they interpreted it in the context of their experience as sojourners and as returning educators. Therefore, whereas the core of the book has focused on the impact of the English language teachers' education on their professional lives, this final chapter presents their reflections on what it has meant to each of them personally.

### Voices from Within

#### *Teacher Fangxue: "My PhD Is My Identity as a Leader"*

His Western education converged with Teacher Fangxue's lifelong view of himself as a person dedicated to his responsibilities as a leader and as a good citizen. His colleagues described him as an optimistic, animated, and energetic 45-year-old. Indeed, Teacher Fangxue lived up to this description because every time we encountered him, we always found him busily and cheerfully running back and forth between his classrooms and his office. His assignment involved teaching non-English-majors language-based classes for 6 hours every week and a master's course in applied linguistics for 4 hours every week. He juggled his teaching load as an associate professor along with his administrative role as a leader in his department while also undertaking a full research agenda.

The result of his dedication, Teacher Fangxue asserted, was the enjoyment he received from being able to fulfill his leadership and citizenry duties. His career decision to take on English-language education and then to pursue a graduate degree in a Western institution was in line with his commitment to serve where he was needed most. Growing up, Teacher Fangxue had excelled in math, but because there were few English teachers in his home town, he set aside his own interests and responded to the urging of his high school principal and local government officials to work toward becoming an English teacher. Thus, fully funded by his province, he majored in English at a local teachers' college and later in the capital city. After obtaining his bachelor's degree, Teacher Fangxue taught English language and English literature at the junior high school level for several years before advancing to the university level. Despite immersing himself in a field that was not his first choice, Teacher Fangxue committed himself to his profession as an English teacher with an ardent sense of mission that revealed his deep sense of dedication to his students' learning, which he regarded as a journey they would take together:

> I have a responsibility to take my students to where they are eager to go, and to answer all kinds of curious questions. I also have an obligation to help them when they face problems. Overall, I see myself as their life-long guide on trips we take together. Before the start of each trip, I try to think of how I can do it better than the last time. When sightseeing begins, I try to arouse their interest with unique information to satisfy their curiosity. That way, if we are to see a mountain, I would like for them to be eager to explore it so that I could lead them to the highest peak to get a good view.
>
> *(Teacher Fangxue, interview, May 22, 2009)*

After 11 years of teaching and making a comfortable living with his wife and child, Teacher Fangxue pulled up stakes to respond one more time to the call of duty, this time in response to his institution's initiative to improve teacher quality by increasing the number of faculty with graduate degrees. He was the first in his province to pursue a PhD, which he achieved after eight long years in the United States, during which time he did not return to China.

Teacher Fangxue said that his time away was time well-spent and worth the sacrifice. He was very proud of his experiences abroad and was always pleased to make people aware of his educational background by bringing it up, especially when introduced to new acquaintances. In addition to providing Teacher Fangxue with immense confidence and pride in his profession, his Western education earned him respect and trust among colleagues and community members as a leader with new and democratic ideas. They were more inclined to listen to him when they knew of his international experience. Moreover, his overseas experience raised his stature as well as his own understanding of his work as a teacher above that of his colleagues who were without overseas experience:

> Cultural and political awareness are so deeply embedded in a culture that if someone only studied these aspects of a different society domestically and did not study abroad, they would not be able to understand and acquire them fully.

*(Teacher Fangxue, interview, May 22, 2009)*

As enthusiastic as he was about his Western education, and despite his whole-hearted commitment to his students' learning, Teacher Fangxue, however, was lukewarm about his subject area because he regarded English as only a tool and said that he just "liked" but not "loved" the English language. Similarly, he regarded being a professor of English as an occupation rather than a calling. What was more important to him at a personal level was that the Western PhD reaffirmed his belief in himself as a responsible and dedicated steward who could garner a following and have a significant impact on his community. With that in mind, Teacher Fangxue decided, despite invitations to serve elsewhere, to return to his former university and department. His leadership skills were quickly recognized, and soon after his return, he was promoted to the position of Vice Dean, for which he thanked his Western studies:

> My Western education gave me precious capital, and I am admired and respected for it both as a teacher and a leader. I have a responsibility to keep because of it.

*(Teacher Fangxue, interview, May 22, 2009)*

### Teacher Lichang: "I Am Still Invisible"

As the highest performing student in English in her high school graduating class in a small city, Teacher Lichang was already convinced that her future was in language studies. After passing the compulsory National College Entrance Examination to enter college, she entered the university of her choice in a large metropolitan area. However, contrary to Teacher Lichang's expectations that her superior exam performance and proficiency in the English language would continue to make her stand out, she found herself as one of many students on campus with a similar proficiency in the language. This challenging experience of finding herself in increasingly competitive environments was to be repeated during her education and then later in her career as a young professional in her early thirties.

After finding that her skills were not unique and that she faced stiff competition, Teacher Lichang considered it as a personal challenge to excel in English in college despite what she now saw as the disadvantage of her traditional public-school training that was focused on grammar-translation in classes that were textbook-, teacher-lecture-, and exam-based. Because of her dedicated efforts, Teacher Lichang was successful in attaining a bachelor's degree in a brief amount of time and was quickly hired as an English instructor right after graduation by a midsized provincial college, where she was among the very few who were well-qualified to teach English. However, before she could establish herself professionally in this college, it was acquired by a prestigious comprehensive university, and again, instead of standing out, Teacher Lichang became a part of a large cadre of proficient English-language professionals. At that point, Teacher Lichang became resigned to accepting her ordinary status and began to view teaching English only as a means to make a living rather than to make a mark in the profession as someone with sought after skills.

Rallying from these early disappointments, Teacher Lichang continued to pursue opportunities to create a niche for herself. Realizing that none of her colleagues had a background in language teaching pedagogy, she chose this direction, which provided her with new motivation and the goal of studying abroad to gain expertise in in a field that was underdeveloped at home:

> I wanted to take some courses such as teaching English as a second language. I never had any professional training in teaching English, especially theoretical and systematic training. Like my other colleagues, except for one course called Teaching Methods during undergraduate study, we never had any professional training. So I feel that, as a teacher, I would do well in my profession by getting pedagogy training.

> *(Teacher Lichang, interview, May 24, 2009)*

Having won a national fellowship, Teacher Lichang could choose among several programs abroad, including opportunities in the United States, but chose to pursue a master's degree in New Zealand. Her classes included those on language teaching methodology, classroom management, and curriculum design, and she was able to take courses from well-known scholars in the field such as Rod Ellis. Excited to return home with renewed energy and knowledge, Teacher Lichang soon faced another disappointment when she found the reception less than what she had hoped for:

> The majority of teachers in my department did not have an opportunity to go abroad. I felt I had to hide my overseas experience. I did not want to hurt other teachers or make them jealous. I seldom talked about my Western learning experience. Actually, nobody except me in my school had studied TESOL. I was really the most knowledgeable person in that

area of study, and I really wanted to showcase my knowledge in front of my colleagues, but of course, I could not.

(Teacher Lichang, interview, May 24, 2009)

Due to the sensitivity of the situation, Teacher Lichang took a backseat with what she brought back from the West and focused instead on working with care and humility on her relationship with her colleagues:

> Though I learned a lot, I could never *teach* my colleagues my ideas. Every teacher has his or her own expertise.... My professional knowledge may be more than theirs, but I may not be as experienced as they are or better than they are in terms of teaching methods. I can also learn from their teaching experiences and I try to let them know I want to learn.

(Teacher Lichang, interview, May 24, 2009)

During our interview with her, she was excited to talk about a recent meeting with three locally trained teachers during which they prepared classes together. Although she was not able to explicitly share her Western-trained knowledge, she was excited to be able to engage with them and to be accepted as a colleague.

Despite the limitations she felt in her interactions with fellow teachers, Teacher Lichang did share her Western-based experiences and knowledge with her students. The joy she derived from teaching was evident in her willingness to teach courses that others avoided and she carried a heavy teaching load. As we mentioned earlier, she was teaching a 6-hour intensive English class on a campus which was an hour's drive from the main campus of her university. Teacher Lichang also volunteered to teach an 8-hour class at another university. Students in her classes expressed to us how much they enjoyed the stories that she brought back from New Zealand. Several also noticed her professional demeanor, expressed in the way she dressed formally in comparison to other teachers. Teacher Lichang said she was emulating her New Zealand professors, whose formal attire while teaching demonstrated a sense of professionalism and seriousness about teaching that she wanted her students to see in her self-presentation:

> I may not dress as formally as Westerners, but I would never wear jeans to teach now. I really cannot stand the way some Chinese teachers dress when they teach.... Overseas, they had strict requirements on the way you dress for different occasions, formal and informal. Your appearance is important if you want to be taken seriously.

(Teacher Lichang, interview, May 24, 2009)

But she still felt she had to suppress much of what she had gained in her studies abroad. Despite the good relationships she was able to maintain with colleagues and her students' receptiveness, Teacher Lichang expressed the following lament:

> I do not have an opportunity to have my voice heard by my colleagues. I offered opinions but they ignored them. The leaders are not supportive and others do not care. My Western learning experience did not bring me any change in terms of my position in the school. I am as invisible as before.
>
> *(Teacher Lichang, interview, May 24, 2009)*

## Teacher Hongyue: "Who I Am Speaks Louder than My Educational Background"

One of the distinguishing features about Teacher Hongyue, a 40-year-old professional and Dean of her department, was her strong sense of self. She felt her educational background and her experiences in the West reinforced her personal values. These included personal responsibility and independence, which were prevailing tenets in her expectations of herself and of others.

Among possible places to study in the West, Teacher Hongyue decided that a PhD program in Australia was the right choice for her mainly because of the opportunity for independent study it provided. She was not required to take any courses except for two training sessions on research methods. She was able to choose courses to audit that she felt could support her knowledge as she conducted her research. Teacher Hongyue liked the Australian system because it allowed her to chart her own path and gave her the freedom to seek out what she needed to improve her work.

It was also clear from her reflections that she was proud of the way she took charge of the direction of her education by taking on challenges and dealing with her own problems:

> The classes I attended were all in English. Professors did not watch their speaking speed. If a student had problems with the language, he had to find ways to solve them by himself. The general feeling was that, "You came to study in this country, and you have the responsibility to deal with the language." I am proud to say that I survived that challenge on my own.
>
> *(Teacher Hongyue, interview, July 19, 2009)*

Upon her return home to China, Teacher Hongyue reiterated her personal values in the way she carried out her duties as an administrator. When asked whom she would prefer to hire in her department, given the choice between a locally and a Western-trained staff member, Teacher Hongyue said she preferred the latter if everything else was equal. However, she also stressed that Western experience should not in itself be a reason for hiring the teacher but should be coupled with the willingness and ability of the individual to act independently:

> If two teachers are in the same situation and both are qualified, I am more willing to hire the one with overseas experience.... But it is up to their ability too. Some teachers come back well-trained overseas but they are incapable of taking action on their own.... It depends on the person.
>
> *(Teacher Hongyue, interview, July 19, 2009)*

There was no doubt that Teacher Hongyue held her overseas education in high regard and was proud of her achievements. Her statements also suggested that as an administrator she would encourage other returnees to share the wealth of their experiences. However, she stressed that these experiences should not be the focus of teaching or interactions with colleagues but used in an unobtrusive way to enrich both:

> You do not need to show it off because it was part of your experience. It should be demonstrated through your teaching activities, but not something that you use to put people and colleagues down. I do not think this is necessary.... I also believe that my colleagues and students will notice my Western education gradually and I will share my experience with them if they ask me. Students especially admire their teachers who have studied abroad. But I do not want them to focus on that. Instead, I want them to pay attention to what and how I am teaching them.
>
> *(Teacher Hongyue, interview, July 19, 2009)*

Finally, what was most important to her personally was that her Western education gave her "a clear mind" about who she was as a person:

> People may admire my experience or they may envy it. Either way they have a different view of me. I am not worried about people's thoughts or expectations. I am confident in myself because I know who I am. I am a Chinese woman with a Western doctorate. I have brought something new back, and I do things differently.
>
> *(Teacher Hongyue, interview, July 19, 2009)*

## *Teacher Meiling: "Western Learning Opened Many Windows of My Heart"*

For Teacher Meiling, Western education was part of a maturing process, which led to her finding herself and a self-defined path for her future. Her early experiences with English began with the influences of her father, who was a professor of English literature and linguistics and taught her English from an early age. He also persuaded her to major in English for her bachelor's degree at a provincial teacher's university. Upon graduation, she became a university teacher but because she was quite young at that point, sometimes younger than her students, she was mentored heavily by her senior colleagues, who provided her with specific directions and resources to teach.

In addition, Teacher Meiling's father followed her career very closely and advised that, after 3 years as an English teacher, she needed to add a master's degree from a university abroad to her qualifications. He contacted his colleagues at a large northern university in the United States, where he had spent time as a visiting scholar, and obtained their support for his daughter's application and acceptance into the university.

Upon arrival at the U.S. university, Teacher Meiling, for the first time, found herself on her own, far away from parental guidance at home and colleagues at work. She found the experience invaluable:

> The experience of going to the U.S. is the most precious one for me in my whole life; it had the greatest influence on me. I had time to be on my own, to really calm down, to be quiet; it was different than when I was in China where I felt every day I was on a tight schedule, busy rushing here and there, listening to this and that person. I felt I was not able to "sink down" to think carefully about things by myself. Being in the U.S. opened many windows of my heart.

*(Teacher Meiling, interview, August 21, 2009)*

As Teacher Meiling's proficiency in English increased, there were also changes in her understanding of ways of thinking and understanding. She was particularly drawn to issues of diversity and ethnicity. She was also able to search for and identify areas other than English-language education that appealed to her and that enhanced her appreciation of multiple perspectives. These led her to change her academic focus and pursue studies in adult education, taking such classes as adult curriculum and instruction and informational literacy for adults. The time away in the United States also enabled Teacher Meiling to reflect on what she wanted from her teaching rather than having to justify whether it was Chinese or Western to others, which she viewed as futile:

> Locally trained teachers would think that my classes lacked lecturing and content, whereas Western teachers might think that they were not interactive enough. It is not useful to have to think about these labels, and I would prefer to focus on where I want to take students to.
>
> *(Teacher Meiling, interview, August 21, 2009)*

The time overseas also resulted in Teacher Meiling reassessing her career. Although she returned to the same university to teach, she surprised everyone, including her father, when she declared she no longer wanted to be an English teacher. Because her new goal in teaching was to motivate students to use their college education as a stepping stone to real outcomes in their lives, she began teaching in the School of Adult Education and Vocational Studies. In this new school, she helped students align their education with their career goals by teaching subjects such as public administration and management in both Chinese and English. She now saw English not as a subject to be learned by itself but as a means to expand thought and to gain access to new ideas. To strengthen her expertise in this area, Teacher Meiling is now pursuing a PhD in education as her next step in life:

> My experience in America enabled me to mature. It has made me think actively and deeply about what my students are really learning and getting from my class. Even though we might not solve all problems, we can think about options and not just accept what is given to us.... My Western education has also given me a picture of what I want to do in the future. As a 30-year-old adult, I feel comfortable saying that I have new tools to think with and new ways to grow. I am special because of it.
>
> *(Teacher Meiling, interview, August 21, 2009)*

Confucius reputedly once said that one must climb a mountain to see what is below. In other words, only through the hard work of progressing upward will one be rewarded with understanding of where one has been and where one is going. In the case of these Western-trained Chinese English language teachers, critical reflection on their past and present experiences were the hard work that they undertook. They were rewarded with an accurate view of where their Western education had brought them and where it might take them further down the road.

# GLOSSARY

**211/985:** List of highest ranking Chinese universities including Peking, Tsinghua, Beijing Normal, Shanghai Jiao Tong, and Zhejiang. The Chinese government gives funding preference to these elite universities to support projects that develop Chinese culture overall and improve the country's international reputation.

**Activity theory:** Activity theory maps the social influences and relationships involved in networks of human activity. The defining components to the theory include the following: *subject* refers to an individual or groups of individuals taking an action; *instruments* are the symbolic or material artifacts that mediate the action through their use; *object* is defined as the problem space or the target toward which the action is directed; *rules* refer to the guiding principles regulating the actions and interactions in the community within which they occur; and finally, *division of labor* takes account of the different roles and responsibilities of the community members in an activity system (Engeström, 1999).

**Appropriation:** As a key concept in activity theory, appropriation is defined as "a process through which a person adopts the pedagogical tools available for use in particular social settings ... and through this process internalizes ways of thinking endemic to specific cultural practices" (Grossman, Smagorinksy, & Valencia, 1999, p. 15). We interpreted this concept in this book as the Chinese English language teachers taking ownership of the communicative language teaching (CLT) approach and its principles by incorporating and juxtaposing them with the norms and practices of their schools and the larger Chinese social setting.

**Backbone teachers (*mófàn jiàoshī*):** Also known as model teachers, they are those teachers that are most experienced in a particular subject area, and may also have won the most teaching awards. The teachers might also be the head teachers in mandated teacher research groups known as the jiàoyánzŭ. These backbone teachers can also be designated as mentors to new teachers to provide them with individual support for as long as they need it.

**Chinese characteristics (jiàn quán chōng mǎn huó lì de jiào yù jī zhì):** This is an expression commonly used to indicate that all reforms and innovations will be shaped to accord with the present Chinese sociocultural, economic, and political context. In other words, reforms are to align with developments in the outside world while keeping in mind that the central government holds the reins tightly.

**Chinese language teaching methods, traditional:** Many English-language students in China have an analytical knowledge of the language in its written form but even after many years of study have poor ability to speak it or understand it in spoken form. This is thought to be the result of the traditional English language teaching methods in China, a combination of the grammar-translation and audiolingual methods characterized by explicit and systematic instruction in grammar, extensive analysis of linguistic details and patterns, emphasis on translation, and strong reliance on memorization and repetition.

**Chinese Scholarship Council (CSC):** This is the official national body in charge of overseeing rules, regulations, and the dispensing of governmental scholarships in China.

**Choral reading:** This is a common practice in Chinese English-language classrooms. Students either stand or sit to read together passages from texts. It is seen as a way to lower the level of apprehension for struggling students while creating opportunities for all students to participate.

**Collaboration:** Collaboration takes place when teachers work together because they share a joint vision and trust, and there is effective leadership that supports the collaboration and formal procedures that make the collaboration possible (D'Amour, 1997).

**College English Test (CET-4):** This is a national test for English as a foreign language. The purpose is to ensure that Chinese university students meet the requirements of the National College English teaching syllabuses.

**Communicative competence:** Communicative competence is core to the communicative language teaching (CLT) approach. Originally conceived by Dell Hymes in 1972, the notion was further developed by Canale and Swain (1980) to include sociolinguistic, discourse, strategic, and grammatical competencies. Sociolinguistic competence consists of learners' ability to use the language appropriately in social situations; discourse competence refers to their ability to combine grammar and meaning to express themselves in new, different, and fluent ways; strategic competence is the use of verbal and nonverbal strategies to cope with challenges of communication;

and grammatical competency is the accurate and effective use of the features and rules of language.

**Content-based language instruction (CBI):** Crandall and Tucker (1990) define CBI as "an approach to language instruction that integrates the presentation of topics or tasks from subject matter classes (e.g., math, social studies) within the context of teaching a second or foreign language" (p. 187).

**Deng Xiaoping's 1978 modernization and open door policy:** Chairman Deng is credited with starting China's path to modernization. The crux of the policy was the reform of the Chinese economic system by opening its markets to the outside world.

**Englishes:** Kachru (1992) argues that second language teaching as a field should move away from idealized native speaker norms in both language and culture toward a concept of English language communicative competence that reflects "the reality of the uses and users of English" (p. 362). This is because ownership of the English language has moved beyond the mainstream of North America, Australia, the United Kingdom, and New Zealand, and English is spoken in many other countries, each with its own unique features that derives from the individual and different cultures.

**Freeman and Johnson's tripartite teacher knowledge base framework (1998):** This framework situates teachers' knowledge base in the nexus of (a) teachers' experiences as learners; (b) the nature of schools and schooling; and (c) the nature of language teaching.

**Glocalization:** The term glocalization, which literally means "global localization," popularized by sociologist Robertson in the 1990s, emphasizes that the globalization of a product is more likely to succeed when the product or service is adapted specifically to each locality or culture it is marketed in. Robertson describes glocalization as "the simultaneity, the co-presence of both universalizing and particularizing tendencies" (1997, p. 4).

**Human agency:** Ahearn (2001) provisionally refers to agency as the "socioculturally mediated capacity to act" (p. 112), capturing a person's capability, as an individual or group member, to initiate and take responsibility for an action while emphasizing how agency "mediates and is mediated by the sociocultural context" (van Lier, 2008, p. 172).

**i+1:** Krashen's (1988) comprehensible input theory where "i" stands for input and "1" is one level above and beyond language learners' competency. The ideal of language teaching, according to Krashen, is to provide input that is comprehensible to learners but that, at the same time, challenges them to strive to learn and to take their competency to the next level. He theorizes that motivation and interest in language learning are sustained that way.

**Imposter syndrome:** A syndrome Llurda (2005) associated with teachers who are nonnative speakers of English (NNESTs) that is associated with feelings of inadequacy, inauthenticity, self-doubt, and low self-esteem. In a world that overvalues teachers who are native speakers of English (NESTs; Bernat, 2008), research on the identity and capability of NNESTs helps them to overcome it.

**Indigenous epistemology:** H. Shin's (2006, p. 148) interpretation of the epistemology appears in her work on the colonial legacy and its extension into the classroom where English as a second language is taught. According to Shin, postcolonial language pedagogy, influenced by indigenous epistemology, always questions the established and external assumptions, prioritizes local knowledge, and never provides a one-size-fits-all teaching method.

**Internalization, transformation, ZPD, and mediation:** Johnson and Golombek (2003) argue that sociocultural theory is a useful framework to explain teacher learning in terms of these key components: First, in internalization and transformation, an individual moves back and forth between external and internal activities which transform them and can only be understood in terms of each other. In this process, "a person's activity is initially mediated by other people or cultural artifacts but later comes to be controlled by the person as he or she appropriates resources to regulate his or her own activities" (p. 731). Second, the mediation occurs in what Vygotsky (1978) defined as the zone of proximal development (ZPD), which suggests that people can advance through collaboration with other more capable individuals and with the help of cultural resources.

*Jiàoyánzŭ:* Translated as "teacher research groups," they are essential in Chinese public schools where much of the in-service teacher professional development (PD) is school-based and involves teachers working together in these groups under the guidance of senior and experienced teachers. Each group can consist of six to eight teachers, including a head teacher assigned by the principal.

**Knowledge-for-practice, knowledge-in-practice, knowledge-of-practice:** Cochran-Smith and Lytle (1999, p. 24) make a distinction between these three types of knowledge that govern teacher education programs. In knowledge-for-practice, students of teaching are to acquire formal knowledge and theory generated by university-based researchers to be used in classrooms to improve teaching. In knowledge-in-practice, it is assumed that the students learn best from probing into and reflecting upon the work of expert teachers and their practical knowledge of curriculum decision making and design of classroom interactions. In knowledge-of-practice, however, Cochran-Smith and Lytle blur the distinction between the two by asserting that teachers are the epicenters of their expertise who are not only informed by and transform knowledge but also generate new knowledge.

*Lăoshī:* The Mandarin term for "people of old and deep wisdom." It is an honorific used as a sign of respect after teachers' family names. The title is also used with other and mostly older individuals, for the same purpose.

**Methodological dogmatism:**    In this book, Reid's (1995, p. 3) phrase is used in relation to Western-based language teaching methods, particularly those labeled "communicative" (D. Liu, 1998). Being viewed as a Holy Grail, the methods appear in virtually every reform movement. Those who question them are usually stigmatized as "traditional" or "backward" (Kubota, 1998, p. 407), labels often applied to those who struggle to reconcile the demands and expectations of these methods with the vastly different learning traditions, cultural expectations, and policies in their own teaching contexts.

**National Economic and Social Development (NESD) Plan (2011–2015):**    The 12th 5-Year National Plan (NESD), endorsed by the People's Republic of China's (PRC) National Congress in March of 2011. It represents a seismic shift from the previous 11 plans that started in 1953. Its goal is to achieve China's transition from being dependent on other countries through its exports to increasing consumption from within its populace of 1.3 billion (Roach, 2011).

**Native speaker fallacy:**    Phillipson (1992) debunks the perception that native speakers (NESTs) by default are superior language teachers of their mother tongue. According to him, among other things, NNESTs, as successful second language learners themselves, have complementary abilities, and at times, even the upper hand in teaching as they may have more insight into what it takes to learn a language other than their own.

**Nonnative English speaking teachers (NNESTs):**    These are teachers who are nonnative speakers of English (NNESTs) and who now comprise the majority of the workforce (80%) in English language classrooms across the globe (Braine, 2010). This predominance is dramatically illustrated by comparing the number of Chinese English language teachers (2 million; Braine, 2010) to the number of certified U.S. teachers of English-language learners (150,000) (Quality Counts, 2009), a quarter of whom are themselves nonnative speakers of English.

**Outline of the National Long-Term and Short-Term Education Reform and Development Plan (2010–2020):**    In comparison to the National Economic and Social Development (NESD), the "Outline" (gāng yào), provides strategic planning and specific guidance. The thrust of the plan is human resource development through education. The Outline's other priorities include education being guaranteed in the national budget, as key in reform and innovation, essential to social stability and equality, and necessary for quality maintenance.

**Postmethod era:**    In this current era, Kumaravadivelu (2006a) calls for an end to teaching models in language teacher education programs regardless of whether they are (a) language-centered methods (e.g., audiolingual), (b) student-centered methods (e.g., communicative language teaching), or (c) learning-centered methods (e.g., natural approach). According to Kumaradivelu, all are flawed in their own ways as evidenced by "ambiguous usage and application, exaggerated claims by proponents and the gradual erosion of their utilitarian value" (p. 162). Above all, Kumaravadivelu points out that teachers' local knowledge is critical and its utility has long been ignored where the concept of "method" is concerned.

**Problematization:** This is a process of evaluating what has been taken for granted. In terms of the Chinese teachers whose work and ideas are discussed in this book, it is the problematization of the saliency of the principles and methods of communicative language teaching (CLT) in the Chinese context in particular, and the assumed "goodness" of all aspects of their Western education in general.

**Process writing:** Process writing is focused on students' communication and expression of ideas. There are multiple steps in the approach including pre-writing, focusing on ideas, and evaluating, structuring, and editing. Peers provide feedback at each of the stages.

**Professional development:** We refer to professional development as consisting of individuals' participation in language teacher education programs either to prepare themselves for or to further their careers as language teachers. These programs can be characterized by the types of knowledge that they are designed to help students acquire.

**Public English Test System (PETS):** Developed by the Chinese Ministry of Education, this is an English test available to all who wish to assess their English language proficiency.

**Realia:** These consist of authentic materials readily available in the media and real-life examples from newspapers, magazines, government publications, and even academic journals. Instead of resorting to a single textbook to be used by students, language teachers use these materials which contain information about current events and social, economic, political, and educational topics of interest.

**Reclaiming the local:** In his edited book, Reclaiming the Local in Language Policy and Practice, Canagarajah (2005) prioritizes the local amidst the global. Such prioritization is needed to challenge the assumption that only Western-based knowledge and practices (particularly in language teaching and learning) are universally relevant and can be applied in all places.

**Rules Educator Preparation and Accountability (REPA II):** Under the leadership of the former Indiana State Superintendent of Public Instruction, Tony Bennett, The Indiana Board of Education pushed through new teacher licensure rules in 2012–2013. Among the most controversial elements of the new rules is the requirement for noneducation majors to only take a test to qualify for a teaching license. The newly elected Superintendent, Glenda Ritz, opposes the rules and her supporters argue a test is insufficient and that pedagogical knowledge and higher education are critical foundations for effective teachers. The new rules, they charge, deprofessionalize teachers and their expertise. REPA II thus is still in limbo in Indiana at the time of writing this book.

**Scaffolding:**  Vygotsky (1978) defines "scaffolding" as the social interaction between experts and novices during which the former engage in supportive behaviors and create supportive environments for the latter to acquire skills and knowledge at a higher competency level than they would on their own.

**Sea turtles (*hǎi guī*):**  Sea turtles is a term used to refer to Chinese students who have returned home from studying overseas. A statement from the Chinese Ministry of Education (CMoE; 2012), reports that from the beginning of the open door policy in 1978 and 2011, a total of 2,245,100 students pursued their education abroad, of whom 818,400 sea turtles or Chinese students overseas had returned home.

**Second language acquisition (SLA) theories:**  These are theories of how second languages are learned and acquired such as the universal theory of language learning in which it is theorized that all humans have the innate capacity to learn languages and that there are common language universals that define all human languages.

**Sense of plausibility:**  Instead of seeking good and bad methods, Prabhu (1990) encourages teachers to analyze their teaching according to whether "it is active, alive, or operational enough to create a sense of involvement for both the teacher and the student" (p. 173). The result of this analysis will be the teacher's sense of plausibility.

**Sociocultural theory:**  This is a Vygotskian-inspired perspective that asserts that our own learning and development are informed and transformed by our experiences in the communities in which we work and live. Criticizing the concept of context-independent cognition, Vygotsky stressed that people learn and develop their cognition and unique ways of thinking through participating in social activities and interacting in cultural contexts. This sociocultural perspective proposes that human thinking and behaviors cannot be understood by looking at the individual in isolation but rather in the contexts of politics, culture, and history.

**Sociocultural turn:**  In the volume celebrating TESOL Quarterly's 40th anniversary, Johnson (2006) describes the sociocultural turn as an epistemological shift in the field of teaching English as a second language "from behaviorist, to cognitive, to situated, social and distributed views of human cognition" (p. 236). From this perspective, teacher learning and development are viewed as "lifelong and emerging out of and through experiences in social contexts" (Johnson, 2006, p. 239).

**Socioprofessionals:**  This is a conception of teachers whose learning and knowledge are embedded in their participation in social practices

(Freeman, 2009, p. 15). In this regard, Freeman has recast the scope of the professional development of second-language teachers to encompass what he calls substance, engagement, and outcomes (p. 15). "Substance" alters the traditional conception of "content," which traditionally refers to the disciplinary skills and knowledge teachers should learn, by also including their participation in the activities within the intellectual, physical, and social settings in which learning and teaching take place.

**Stimulus recall:** This approach as described in this book is one whereby teachers and researchers viewed together the formers' videotaped teaching. Teachers recalled and reflected on what they remembered in terms of their intention behind their instruction and what they were planning to achieve at certain moments in the classroom as well as their overall instructional objectives. Reflections in these recalls usually touched upon what was successful and what could be further improved. The reflections and discussions were mostly teacher- rather than researcher-led.

**Student-centeredness:** In a student-centered classroom, students' readiness for autonomy is acknowledged. In addition, they are seen not simply as learners but as managers of their learning. Thus, they are not regarded as passive knowledge receivers; instead, students are encouraged to negotiate meaning in their interactions with peers as well as teachers in the classrooms.

**Test of English as a Foreign Language (TOEFL):** This is a language test for international students who intend to study in U.S. universities. The TOEFL-IBT is the latest Internet-based version of the test.

*Zhōng guó*: The Mandarin term for "The Middle Kingdom," as China is known to the Chinese people. Historically, it can also refer to the "center of civilization" denoting the importance of the location where a Chinese emperor was situated.

# REFERENCES

Achinstein, B. (2002). Conflict amid community: The micropolitics of teacher collaboration. *Teachers College Record, 104*(3), 421–455.

Ahearn, L. M. (2001). Language and agency. *Annual Review of Anthropology, 30,* 109–137.

Alptekin, C. (2002). Towards intercultural communicative competence in ELT. *ELT Journal, 56*(1), 57–64.

APCO Worldwide. (2010, December 10). *China's 12th Five Year Plan: How it actually works and what is in store for the next five years.* Retrieved from http://apcoworldwide.com/content/PDFs/Chinas_12th_Five-Year_Plan.pdf

Bailey, K. M., Curtis, A., & Nunan, D. (1998). Undeniable insights: The collaborative use of three professional development practices. *TESOL Quarterly, 32*(3), 546–556.

Bax, S. (2003a). The end of CLT: A context approach to language teaching. *ELT Journal, 57*(3), 278–287.

Bax, S. (2003b). Bringing context and methodology together. *ELT Journal, 57*(3), 295–296.

Bernat, E. (2008). Beyond beliefs: Psycho-cognitive, sociocultural and emergent ecological approaches to learner perceptions in foreign language acquisition. *The Asian EFL Journal, 10*(3). Retrieved from http://www.asian-efl-journal.com/September_08_eb.php

Bradsher, K. (2013, January, 16). Next-made-in-China boom: College graduates. *The New York Times.* Retrieved from http://www.nytimes.com/2013/01/17/business/chinas-ambitious-goal-for-boom-in-college-graduates.html?pagewanted=all&_r=0

Brady, B., & Gulikers, G. (2004). Enhancing the MA in TESOL practicum course for non-native English-speaking student teachers. In L. Kamhi-Stein (Ed.), *Learning and teaching from experience: Perspectives on nonnative English-speaking professionals* (pp. 206–229). Ann Arbor: Michigan University Press.

Braine, G. (2010). *Non-native speaker teachers: Research, pedagogy and professional growth.* New York, NY: Routledge.

Branscombe, N. A., Goswami, D., & Schwartz, J. (Eds.). (1992). *Students teaching, teachers learning.* Portsmouth, NH: Boynton/Cook-Heinemann.

Brutt-Griffler, J., & Samimy, K. (1999). What can a TESOL program offer to their "nonnative" professionals? *TESOL NNEST Newsletter, 1*(1), 8–9.

Burnaby, B., & Sun, Y. L. (1989). Chinese teachers' views of Western language teaching: Context informs paradigms. *TESOL Quarterly, 23*(2), 219–238.

Canagarajah, A. S. (Ed.). (2005). *Reclaiming the local in language policy and practice.* Mahwah, NJ: Erlbaum.

Canale, M., & Swain, M (1980). Theoretical basis of communicative approaches to second language learning and testing. *Applied Linguistics, 1,* 1–47.

Carless, D. (2008). Student use of the mother tongue in the task-based classroom. *Language Teaching Journal, 62*(4), 331–338.

China Direct. (2011, May 11). *China's Twelfth Five Year Plan (2011–2015).* Retrieved from http://cbi.typepad.com/china_direct/2011/05/chinas-twelfth-five-new-plan-the-full-english-version.html

Chinese Ministry of Education (CMoE). (2003). *National curriculum standards album: English curriculum standards.* http://www.being.org.cn/ncs/eng/eng02.htm

Chinese Ministry of Education (CMoE). (2012). *Demographic statistics of overseas Chinese students in 2011.* Retrieved from http://www.moe.gov.cn/publicfiles/business/htmlfiles/moe/s5987/201202/130328.html.

Chinese Scholarship Council (CSC). (2012a, October 15). *CSC scholarship plan for 2013.* Retrieved from http://www.csc.edu.cn/News/4fa022c7254648ffa2be9ed8dacbf8bb.shtml.

Chinese Scholarship Council (CSC). (2012b, November 15). *2013 CSC Scholarship Programs Introduction.* Retrieved from http://www.csc.edu.cn/Chuguo/c1a98c-0c23074a9a87eff30664149f51.shtml.

Chinese State Council. (2010, July 29). *Chinese education reform and development guideline* (2010–2020). Retrieved from http://www.gov.cn/jrzg/2010-07/29/content_1666937.htm.

Chowdhury, R., & Ha, P. L. (2008). Reflecting on Western TESOL training and communicative language teaching: Bangladeshi teachers' voices. *Asia Pacific Journal of Education, 28,* 305–316.

Cochran-Smith, M., & Lytle, S. L. (1999). Relationships of knowledge and practice: Teacher learning in communities. *Review of Research in Education, 24,* 249–305.

Cook, V. (1999). Going beyond the native speaker in language teaching. *TESOL Quarterly, 33*(2), 185–209.

Cowan, J., Light, R., Mathews, B., & Tucker, G. (1979). English teaching in China: A recent survey. *TESOL Quarterly, 12*(4), 465–482.

Crandall, J. (2000). Language teacher education. *Annual Review of Applied Linguistics, 20,* 34–55.

Crandall, J., & Tucker, G. R. (1990). Content-based instruction in second and foreign languages. In A. Padilla, H. H. Fairchild, & C. Valadez (Eds.), *Foreign language education: Issues and strategies* (pp. 187–200). Newbury Park, CA: Sage.

Cullen, R. (1994). Incorporating a language improvement component in teacher training programmes. *ELT Journal, 48*(2), 162–172.

D'Amour, D. (1997). *Structuration de la collaboration interprofessionnelle dans les services de santé de première ligne au Québec* [Structuring of interprofessional collaboration in frontline health services in Quebec]. (Unpublished doctoral dissertation). Université de Montréal, Canada.

Ellis, R. (2006). Current issues in the teaching of grammar: An SLA perspective. *TESOL Quarterly, 40*(1), 83–107.

Engeström, Y. (1987). *Learning by expanding: An activity-theoretical approach to developmental research.* Helsinki, Finland: Orienta-Konsultit.

Engeström, Y. (1999). Activity theory and individual and social transformation. In Y. Engeström, R. Miettinen, & R-L. Punamaki (Eds.), *Perspectives on activity theory* (pp. 19–38). Cambridge, England: Cambridge University Press.

Engeström, Y. (2001). Expansive learning at work: Toward an activity theoretical reconceptualization. *Journal of Education and Work, 14*(1), 133–156.

Fan, C. C. (2006). China's Eleventh Five-Year Plan (2006–2010): From "Getting Rich First" to "Common Prosperity." *Eurasian Geography and Economics, 47*(6), 708–723.

Farber, B. (1991). *Crisis in education.* San Francisco, CA: Jossey-Bass.

Fei, Y. S. (2004). An inquiry about strengths and limitations of communicative approach. *Theory and Practice of Education, 24*, 53–54.

Firth, A., & Wagner, J. (1998). SLA property: No trespassing! *Modern Language Journal, 82*(1), 92–94.

Freeman, D. (1991). "To make the tacit explicit": Teacher education, emerging discourse, and conceptions of teaching. *Teaching and Teacher Education, 7*, 439–454.

Freeman, D. (1996). Redefining the relationship between research and what teachers know. In K. M. Bailey & D. Nunan (Eds.), *Voices from the language classroom: Qualitative research in second language education* (pp. 88–115). New York, NY: Cambridge University Press.

Freeman, D. (2009). The scope of second language teacher education. In A. Burns & J. A. Richards (Eds.), *The Cambridge guide to second language teacher education* (pp. 11–19). Cambridge, England: Cambridge University Press.

Freeman, D., & Johnson, K. E. (1998). Reconceptualizing the knowledge-base of language teacher education. *TESOL Quarterly, 32*, 397–417.

Friedman, T. L. (1999). *The Lexus and the olive tree: Understanding globalization.* New York, NY: Farrar, Straus & Giroux.

Govardhan, A. K., Nayar, B., & Sheorey, R. (1999). Do U.S. MATESOL programs prepare students to teach abroad? *TESOL Quarterly, 3*(1), 114–125.

Graddol, D. (2001). The future of English as a European language. *The European English Messenger, 10*(2), 47–50.

Grossman, P. L., Smagorinsky, P., & Valencia, S. (1999). Appropriating tools for teaching English: A theoretical framework for research on learning to teach. *American Journal of Education, 108*(1), 1–29.

Ha, P. L. (2004). University classrooms in Vietnam: Contesting the stereotypes. *ELT Journal, 58*(1), 50–57.

Hai, T., Qiang, N., & Wolff, M. (2004). China's ELS goals: Are they being met? *English Today, 20*(3), 37–44.

Han, Y. (1993). On the teacher (J. G. Luo, Trans.). *English Language Learning, 9*, 56.

Harcher, P. (2012, October 30). Singapore: A Chinese model for democracy. *The Sydney Morning Herald.* Retrieved from http://www.smh.com.au/opinion/politics/singapore-a-model-for-chinese-democracy-20121029-28fkc.html

Harmer, J. (2003). Popular culture, methods, and context. *ELT Journal, 57*(3), 288–294.

He, D., & Zhang, Q. (2010). Native speaker norms and China English: From the perspective of learners and teachers in China. *TESOL Quarterly, 44*(4), 769–789.

He, M. (2000, September 28). English teaching method faces challenge. *China Daily*. Retrieved from http://www.chinadaily.net

Hu, G. (2002). Potential cultural resistance to pedagogical imports: The case of communicative language teaching in China. *Language, Culture and Curriculum, 15*(2), 93–105.

Hu, G. (2003). English language teaching in China: Regional differences and contributing factors. *Journal of Multilingual and Multicultural Development, 24*(4), 290–318.

Hu, G. (2005). English language education in China: Policies, progress, and problems. *Language Policy, 4,* 5–24.

Hui, L. (1997). New bottles, old wine: Communicative language teaching in China. *Forum, 35*(4), 38–48.

Hymes, D. (1972). On communicative competence. *Sociolinguistics,* 53–73.

Jacobs, G. M., & Farrell, T. S. C. (2003). Understanding and implementing the CLT paradigm. *RELC Journal, 34,* 5–30.

Jin, L., & Cortazzi, M. (2006). Changing practices in Chinese cultures of learning: Language, culture and curriculum. *Culture and Curriculum, 19*(1), 5–20.

Johnson, K. E. (2006). The sociocultural turn and its challenges for second language teacher education. *TESOL Quarterly, 40*(1), 235–257.

Johnson, K. E. (2009). *Second language teacher education: A sociocultural perspective.* New York, NY: Routledge.

Johnson, K. E., & Golombek, P. R. (2003). "Seeing" teacher learning. *TESOL Quarterly, 37,* 729–737.

Kachru, B. B. (1990). World Englishes and applied linguistics. *World Englishes, 9*(1), 3–20.

Kachru, B. B. (1992). World Englishes: Approaches, issues and resources. *Language Teaching, 25*(01), 1–14.

Kamhi-Stein, L. (2000). Adapting U.S.-based TESOL education to meet the needs of non-native English speakers. *TESOL Journal, 9*(3), 10–14.

Karavas-Doukas, E. (1996). Using attitude scales to investigate teachers' attitude to the communicative approach. *ELT Journal, 50,* 187–198.

Korthagen, F. A. (2001). *Linking practice and theory: The pedagogy of realistic teacher education.* Mahwah, NJ: Erlbaum.

Kramsch, C., & Sullivan, P. (1996). Appropriate pedagogy. *ELT Journal, 50,* 199–212.

Krashen, S. (1988). *Language acquisition and second language learning.* New York, NY: Prentice Hall.

Kubota, R. (1998). Ideologies of English in Japan. *World Englishes, 17*(3), 295–306

Kumaravadivelu, B. (1993). Maximizing learning potential in the communicative classroom. *ELT Journal, 47,* 12–21.

Kumaravadivelu, B. (2001). Toward a postmethod pedagogy. *TESOL Quarterly, 35,* 537–560.

Kumaravadivelu, B. (2006a). *Understanding language teaching: From method to post-method.* Mahwah, NJ: Erlbaum.

Kumaravadivelu, B. (2006b). TESOL methods: Changing tracks, challenging trends. *TESOL Quarterly, 40,* 59–81.

Lagabaster, D., & Sierra, J. M. (2004). *La observación como instrumento para la mejora de la enseñanza-aprendizaje de la lenguas* [Observation as a tool for improving teaching and learning of languages]. Barcelona, Spain: Editorial Horsori.

Lantolf, J. P. (Ed.). (2000). *Sociocultural theory and second language learning*. Oxford, England: Oxford University Press.

Lantolf, J. P., & Pavlenko, A. (2001). (S)econd (L)anguage (A)ctivity theory: Understanding second language learners as people. In M. P. Breen (Ed.), *Learner contributions to language learning: New directions in research* (pp. 141–158). Essex, England: Pearson Education.

Lantolf, J. P., & Thorne, S. L. (2006). *Sociocultural theory and the genesis of second language development* (Vol. 398). Oxford, England: Oxford University Press.

Li, X. (1984). In defense of the communicative approach. *ELT Journal, 38*, 2–13.

Liao, X. (2000). How communicative language teaching became acceptable in secondary schools in China. *The Internet TESL Journal, 6*(10). Retrieved from http://www.aitech.ac.jp/~iteslj/Articles/Liao-CLTinChina.html

Liao, X. (2004). The need for communicative language teaching in China. *ELT Journal, 58*(3), 270–272.

Lin, L. (2002). English education in present-day China. *Asian/Pacific Book Development, 33*(2), 8–9.

Littlewood, W. (1981). *Communicative language teaching*. Cambridge, England: Cambridge University Press.

Liu, D. (1998). Ethnocentrism in TESOL: Teacher education and the neglected needs of international TESOL students. *ELT Journal, 52*(1), 3–10.

Liu, D. L. (1999). Training non-native TESOL students: Challenges for TESOL teacher education in the west. In G. Braine (Ed.), *Non-native educators in English language teaching* (pp. 197–211). Mahwah, NJ: Erlbaum.

Llurda, E. (2004). Non-native-speaker teachers and English as an international language. *International Journal of Applied Linguistics, 14*(3), 314–323.

Llurda, E. (2005). *Educational linguistics*: Vol. 5. *Non-native language teachers: Perceptions, challenges, and contributions to the profession*. New York, NY: Springer.

Lo, Y. G. (2005). Relevance of knowledge of second language acquisition. In N. Bartels (Ed.), *Applied linguistics and language teacher education* (pp. 135–158). New York, NY: Springer.

Lytle, S. L., & Cochran-Smith, M. (1992). Teacher research as a way of knowing. *Harvard Educational Review, 62*(4), 447–474.

Mahboob, A., Uhrig, K., Hartford, B., & Newman, K. (2001). Children of a lesser English: Nonnative English speakers as ESL teachers in English language programs in the United States. In L. D. Kamhi-Stein (Ed.), *Learning and teaching from experience: Perspectives on non-native English speaking professionals* (pp. 100–120). Ann Arbor: University of Michigan Press.

Maurice, K. (1983). The fluency workshop. *TESOL Newsletter, 17*(4), 29.

McEwan, H., & Bull, B. (1991). The pedagogic nature of subject matter knowledge. *American Educational Research Journal, 28*(2), 316–334.

Medgyes, P. (1986). Queries from a communicative teacher. *ELT Journal, 40*(2), 107–112.

Mohrman, K. (2008). The emerging global model with Chinese characteristics. *Higher Education Policy, 21*, 29–48.

Ng, C., & Tang, E. (1997). Teachers' needs in the process of EFL reform in China—A report from Shanghai. *Perspectives: Working Papers, 9*(1), 63–85.

Open Doors. (2011) *International student enrollment increased by 5 percent in 2010/11*. Retrieved from http://www.iie.org/en/Who-We-Are/News-and-Events/Press-Center/Press-Releases/2011/2011-11-14-Open-Doors-International-Students

Outline of China's National Plan for Medium and Long-Term Education Reform and Development (2010–2020). (2010). Retrieved from https://www.aei.gov.au/news/newsarchive/2010/documents/china_education_reform_pdf.pdf

Ouyang, H. (2000). One-way ticket: A story of an innovative teacher in mainland China. *Anthropology & Education Quarterly, 31*(4), 397–425.

Pavlenko, A. (2003). "I never knew I was a bilingual": Reimagining teacher identities in TESOL. *Journal of Language, Identity, and Education, 2*(4), 251–268.

Pawan, F., & Fan, W. (2013). Sustaining expertise through collaborative/peer-mediated and individual reflections. The experiences of Chinese English language teachers. Manuscript submitted for publication.

Pawan, F., & Groff Thomalla, T. (2005). Making the invisible, visible: A responsive evaluation study of ESL and Spanish language services for immigrants in a small rural county in Indiana. *TESOL Quarterly, 39*(4), 683–705.

Peirce, B. N. (1995). Social identity, investment, and language learning. *TESOL Quarterly, 29*(1), 9–31.

Pennycook, A. (1989). The concept of method, interested knowledge, and the politics of language. *TESOL Quarterly, 23*, 589–618.

Pennycook, A. (1999). Introduction: Critical approaches to TESOL. *TESOL Quarterly, 33*(3), 329–348.

Phillipson, R. (1992). *Linguistic imperialism.* Oxford, England: Oxford University Press.

Prabhu, N. S. (1990). There is no best method—Why? *TESOL Quarterly, 24,* 161–176.

Qing, L. (2004). Analyzing the obstacles in implementing communicative language teaching. *Journal of Education and Career, 9,* 64–65.

Quality Counts, (2009, January 8). *Portrait of a population.* Retrieved from http://www.edweek.org/ew/toc/2009/01/08/index.html

Ramanathan, V. (2006). The vernacularization of English: Crossing global currents to re-dress West-based TESOL. *Critical Inquiry in Language Studies: An International Journal, 3,* 131–146.

Rao, Z. (1996). Reconciling communicative approaches to the teaching of English with traditional Chinese methods. *Research in the Teaching of English, 30*(4), 458–471.

Rao, Z. (2002). Chinese students' perceptions of communicative and non-communicative activities in EFL classroom. *System, 30,* 85–105.

Reid, J. M. (1995). President's message: Let's put the "T" back in TESL/TEFL programs. *TESOL Matters, 5*(6), 3.

Richards, J. C. (2005). Communicative language teaching today. *Southeast Asian Ministers of Education Organization.* Singapore: Regional Language Center.

Richards, J. C. (2009, March, 27). The changing face of TESOL. *Plenary address at the 2009 TESOL Convention in Denver USA.* Retrieved from http://www.tesolmedia.com/videos/convention09/jackrichards.html

Richards, J. C., & Lockhart, C. (1994). *Reflective teaching in second language classrooms.* Cambridge, England: Cambridge University Press.

Roach, S. S. (2011). China's 12th Five-Year Plan: Strategies and tactics. *Morgan Stanley,* 1–10. Retrieved from http://www.morganstanley.com/im/emailers/inst/pdf/China_12th_Five_Year_Plan.pdf

Robertson, R. (1997). Values and globalization: Communitarianism and globality. In

Luiz E. Scares (Ed.), *Cultural pluralism, identity, and globalization* (pp. 73–97). Rio de Janeiro, Brazil: UNESCO and Candido Mendes University.

Ross, H., & Lou, J. (2005). "Glocalizing" Chinese higher education: Groping for stones to cross the river. *Indiana Journal of Global Legal Studies, 12*, 227–250.

San Martín-Rodríguez, L., Beaulieu, M., D'Amour, D., & Ferrada-Videla, M. (2005). The determinants of successful collaboration: A review of theoretical and empirical studies [Supplement 1]. *Journal of Interprofessional Care*, 132–147.

Sato, K., & Kleinsasser, R. C. (1999). Communicative language teaching (CLT): Practical understandings. *The Modern Language Journal, 83*, 494–517.

Sharkey, J. (2004). ESOL teachers' knowledge of context as critical mediator in curriculum development. *TESOL Quarterly, 38*(2), 279–299.

Sharkey, J., & Johnson, K. E. (Eds.). (2003). *The TESOL Quarterly dialogues: Rethinking issues of language, culture, and power*. Alexandria, VA: TESOL.

Shih, M. (1999). More than practicing language: Communicative reading and writing for Asian settings. *TESOL Journal, 8*(4), 20–25.

Shin, H. (2006). Rethinking TESOL from a SOL's perspective: Indigenous epistemology and decolonizing praxis in TESOL. *Critical Inquiry in Language Studies: An International Journal, 3*, 147–167.

Shin, S. J. (2008). Preparing non-native English-speaking ESL teachers. *Teacher Development, 12*(1), 57–65.

Shkedi, A. (2005). *Multiple case narrative: A qualitative approach to studying multiple populations*. Amsterdam, the Netherlands: Benjamins.

Shulman, L. S. (1987). Knowledge and teaching: Foundations of the new reform. *Harvard Educational Review, 57*(1), 1–23.

Stigmar, M. (2010). Scholarship of teaching and learning when bridging theory and practice in higher education. *International Journal for the Scholarship of Teaching and Learning, 4*(2). Retrieved from http://www.georgiasouthern.edu/ijsotl

Sullivan, P. N. (2000). Playfulness as mediation in communicative language teaching in a Vietnamese classroom. In J. P. Lantolf (Ed.), *Sociocultural theory and second language learning* (pp. 115–133). Oxford, England: Oxford University Press.

Sun, G., & Cheng, L. (2002). From context to curriculum: A case study of communicative language teaching in China. *TESL Canada Journal, 19*(2), 67–86.

Swain, M. (1985). A critical look at the communicative language approach. *ELT Journal, 39*(2), 2–12.

van Lier, L. (2008). Agency in the classroom. In J. P. Lantolf & M. E. Poehner (Eds.), *Sociocultural theory and the teaching of second languages* (pp. 163–86). London, England: Equinox.

Vygotsky, I. S. (1978). *Mind in society: The development of higher psychological processes*. Cambridge, MA: Harvard University Press.

Wallace, M. J. (1991). *Training foreign language teachers: A reflective approach*. Cambridge, England: Cambridge University Press.

Wang, H. (2011). *Recent trends in college English teacher development in China*. Paper presented at the Beijing TESOL Conference, Beijing Normal University.

Wenger, E. (1998). *Communities of practice: Learning, meaning and identity*. New York, NY: Cambridge University Press.

Yan, X. F. (2000). Lu Ying Xiang Jiao Ji Jiao Xue Fa Tui Xing De Wen Hua Yin Su [Reasons for the poor implementation of CLT in China: A cultural dimension analysis]. *Foreign Language Teaching Abroad, 1*, 13–16.

Yunnan Normal University (YNU). (2011, December 27). *Notice on printing and distributing Yunnan Normal University 12th Five-Year Plan*, 11–16. Kunming, People's Republic of China: Author.

Zhong, B. L. (1999). Actively promoting teaching method and methodology reform. *Teaching and Teaching Material, 121*(3), 8–10.

Zhou, Y. H. (2001). Observation and discussion of communicative approach and its application in college English teaching. *Journal of Hefei University of Technology, 15*(1), 128–132.

Zhu, Y. (2007). *Culture and self.* Beijing, People's Republic of China: Beijing Normal University Press.

# INDEX